Your Employees Have Quit

They Just Haven't Left

Nine Fundamental Principles to Engage
and Transform Your Workplace Culture

Rich Schlentz

ISBN: 1450590446
ISBN-13: 9781450590440

To Ivy, Taylor and Carley, the three people who have believed in me often before I've believed in myself. Thank you for bringing deep meaning and full engagement to my life and work.

Contents

Acknowledgments

Thank you to the leaders who model what it's like to create and foster engaging cultures. Special appreciation goes to those who allowed me to ask questions and utilize their expert answers in this book: Bret Grieves, Jeff Burkett, Marty Freeman, Mary Cloninger, Todd Herman, Larry Diana, Mark Hyman, Frank Middlebury, and Paolo Chiappina. Also, special thanks to my writing coach, colleague, and friend Jerome Daley: you've patiently coached and guided me so this book, which resided in me, could come out and be published. I'd also like to thank my trusted friends and fellow professionals who took time to edit early writing and tell me the truth in love: Emily Howard, Chris Laney, Nigel Alston, Joey Slepp, Gary Bradt, Jennifer Thomas, Carol Wise, Chris Avis, and Carla Mata-Sprinkles.

CHAPTER ONE

Engage 'Em or Lose 'Em

You can't solve a problem with the same mind that created it.

–Albert Einstein

He was talking, but I couldn't make out his words. Apparently, I was having one of those Charlie Brown moments—you know, the teacher's mouth is moving, yet all the kids hear is, "Wha wha…wha wha…wha wha…"

"I just can't figure out how to motivate our people," he said. The vice president leaned back in his chair and grimaced. "We have clearly articulated the results we're after, but the reports we get back are dismal. Our people just aren't getting it."

"What is it that you most want them to get?" I asked.

"I want them to care about our customers," he responded in exasperation. "I want them to work effectively in teams. I want them to be creative and productive. Am I asking too much of them?"

I could tell that he meant the question to be rhetorical, so I pressed on gamely. "So you're pretty dissatisfied with your employees. How are you trying to shape the culture here?"

He didn't seem to have heard me. "The economy has bitten deeply into our sales numbers, and now we can't seem to keep the customer base we already have. On top of that, our best salespeople keep leaving for competitors, and we have to start over training newbies. Rich, we really need you to bring a full-day workshop to address these issues. When can you come?"

I could tell that, in his mind, he was ready to offload this responsibility to me so he could return to his daily distractions of reports, meetings, and the illusion of "more important things." Simultaneously, it had become clear to me that, although my professional credentials included consultant, speaker, and leadership coach, in reality I had become a hired gun—a training and workshop mercenary.

The vice president wasn't finished yet. He was speaking passionately and eloquently, but I was drifting back into Charlie Brown mode. Snatches of conversation broke through like, "workgroup infighting," "broken lines of communication," and "resistance to change."

"Stop!" I wanted to scream. "I've heard it all before." These conversations are about symptoms, and the recommendations I had been delivering for years were merely masking the pain. There seemed to be little long-term, sustainable change. What we were achieving was a momentary feel-good experience from a motivational workshop or learning experience. It's like treating bronchitis with a cherry cough drop; it tastes good going down, but it doesn't help the infection.

❈ ❈ ❈

I no longer spend my time and my client's money chasing the imposters while ignoring the real issue. The core concern we're facing is disengagement.

❈ ❈ ❈

From here on out, I decided, it's going to be different. The problems global enterprises are facing aren't about poor customer service, lack of teamwork, or slumping sales and profits. The issues are not unresolved conflict, poor change management, deficient communication, or a drop in productivity. The challenges really aren't a lack of motivation, innovation, or inspiration. These are all symptoms of the real problem. I no longer spend my time and my clients' money chasing the imposters while ignoring the real issue. The core concern we're facing is *disengagement*—that's what this book is about: disengagement and how to remedy it. Are you with me?

Disengagement can appear in a number of ways. Recently, I had dinner with a longtime friend of mine, Joey, aka Joey from Jersey. Joey understands and thrives in corporate America. I've always admired his business savvy as he balances analytical and interpersonal skills. He's been a high achiever since graduating from college in the 1980s and earning his MBA while working full time.

Joey is a highly successful senior sales executive with a nationally recognized organization. For five years he has been reporting to a revolving door of ineffective and out-of-touch managers. His team members have been dropping like flies, unable to succeed in an environment muddied by poor communication, lack of clear direction, and a "throw-them-on-the-wall-and-hope-some-stick" hiring mentality. Despite this reality, Joey consistently hits 140 to 150 percent of his yearly sales goals. With this kind of performance, he's a keeper. Yet here's what he said to me over our pasta dinner,

> Rich, guess what…They did it again. I hit one hundred and forty percent of my company sales goals this

year. In response to my ongoing success, they've once again changed the compensation plan and increased my quota so that I'll likely make less money next year. I'm going to stay around until December—that's when I'm fully vested. If I leave beforehand, it's like throwing away money. After that, I'll start looking.

Do you see it? He's planning his exit strategy. He's checked out mentally and emotionally. Joey has quit—he just hasn't left. His company has taken a loyal, high-producing sales executive and created a culture that will diminish his results and send him packing to the competition.

The Core Issue

The first step toward any solution is to name the problem. The problem we're facing is the disengagement of the American workforce. There is plenty of supporting research: just type "research on employee engagement" into your Google search, and you'll receive over half a million hits.

❖ ❖ ❖

The first step toward any solution is to name the problem.

❖ ❖ ❖

Facts to consider:

- Engaged employees average 27 percent less absenteeism than those who are disengaged.
- Business units with a surplus of disengaged employees suffer 31 percent more turnover than those with a critical mass of engaged associates.

- Workgroups with an inordinately high number of disengaged workers lose 51 percent more of their inventory to "shrink" than do those on the other end of the spectrum.
- The workgroups whose disengagement puts them in the bottom quartile of the Gallup database average 62 percent more accidents than the workgroups in the top quartile.
- Higher levels of team engagement equate to 12 percent higher customer scores than those in the bottom tier.
- Engaged teams average 18 percent higher productivity and 12 percent higher profitability.[1]

Simply put, employee engagement is a brilliant business tactic, yet the disengagement crisis is at epidemic proportions. How we respond may determine whether we remain viable as a global business leader. We are a country made up of smart people, and I've often wondered: What if we didn't have all this data? What if we didn't have millions of employee surveys to point out the obvious? What if we only had our ability to observe what's happening within our own organizations? Would we get it?

Paying Attention

After graduating college with a degree in exercise physiology, I co-owned and operated several fitness/wellness centers for fifteen years. As a service for new members, our exercise specialists would conduct fitness assessments. The concept was that the data collected would help our clients determine their current state of fitness or lack thereof. But one day it dawned on me: *this is stupid.*

Prospective members came into our health club for a reason. Most were overly fat and under conditioned. They were fully aware of this reality; that's why they showed up. After spending an hour and a half with one of our experts, we would conclude with the use of our scientific measurement devices and extensive educational certifications that they were indeed overly fat and under conditioned. I recognized that this need to collect data was about us (the fitness professional), not about them (those seeking a solution). What our clients wanted was straightforward—help them make the changes necessary to become active, be healthy, and feel better.

That's where we are with our disengagement issue. You don't need reams of data to recognize that the typical American employee has checked out. You do need to pay attention. Your employees already know and feel it. Can you see it in their eyes and hear it in their voices? The problem is already identified. Here are the sounds of disengagement within your organization. Place a check mark next to comments that you have already heard:

___ I have no clear idea what's expected of me in my role.

___ I don't have the materials or equipment to do my job right.

___ I wish I had the opportunity to utilize my natural strengths and do what I do best.

___ I can't remember the last time someone around here gave me honest and sincere praise or recognition…without wanting something in return.

__ I feel like a number here. Nobody, including my supervisor, really cares about me.

__ I wish I had a mentor at work, someone who took a real interest in supporting and encouraging my development.

__ My opinions and ideas don't seem to count here. I've learned to keep them to myself.

__ Yes, we have a company mission statement, but it means nothing to my colleagues and me.

__ I can't count on my team members to do quality work. They do just enough to get by.

__ I don't have any close relationships at my work. I wish I had a best friend here.

__ I can't recall the last time I had a meaningful conversation about my progress. I don't really know if I'm successful or not. Our "annual reviews" are a waste of time.

__ I feel stagnant. There are really no opportunities to learn and grow.[2]

Reforming the System

Markets change. Technology changes. Your competition changes. Your products change. But the essence of your people hasn't changed. I observe companies that have successfully navigated the rapid changes of markets, technology, competition, and products...and then fail with people. I hear them tell me, "Rich, our biggest challenge is attracting and retaining good people." What's that all about? How can the most challenging area within organizations today be the one thing that has remained virtually the same—people?

It's time to rethink this. Through the ages, there are countless examples of men and women who have helped shift their generation's beliefs. Among them was a German monk, theologian, and university professor named Martin Luther. He questioned the predominant religious "thinkers" of his day. He challenged accepted thoughts about the papacy, salvation, priesthood, repentance, and faith. He tackled some particularly thorny

How can the most challenging area within organizations today be the one thing that has remained virtually the same—people?

issues, and his ideas for change were recorded in 1517 through his Ninety-Five Theses. Because of his contrarian thinking, he was viewed as an outlaw. Yet he is recognized for changing the course of Western civilization, encouraging others to share their doubts about the established church and to protest its ways.[3]

The word that Luther's contemporaries used to describe the endless and necessary process of change and growth is *reforming*. It is the core belief that all current thoughts, ideas, and actions are subject to be revisited, rethought, and reworked. As a leader, you are in a position to reform. This should not stem from ego. This is not about "right or wrong." It is about your human design. You have the choice to be a bystander in this great story of life, or you can play an interactive role in coauthoring your individual journey, leaving a unique mark on your personal civilization. It is time to accept your calling to reform the way your company or department thinks about and responds to the issue of employee engagement.

The Beatles sang, "You say you want a revolution. Well, you know, we all want to change the world."[4] Revolution. Reformation. They both emerge from a deep belief that things can and should be different. And the results are the same—change. Change within you and change around you. Both are scary, requiring courage and passion. Don't worry about changing *the* world; let's concentrate on changing *your* world.

It's important that those looking to you for leadership and direction believe you are in touch with their world. They want to believe you have a real sense of what they are experiencing and feeling. They desire your awareness, followed up with meaningful and purposeful action that addresses their plight. A Chinese proverb says, "The best time to plant a tree was twenty years ago. The next best time is today." So it is with creating an engaging work culture. Today is the right time to begin planting.

What Kind of Leaders Are We Talking About?

Good question. Both leadership and engagement are far-reaching topics. We can refer to leaders in the traditional sense: those who bear the title of supervisor, manager, director, vice president, or owner. There are also situations in which people lead without authority, such as peer to peer. A person can lead an idea or as part of a project team. I've coached clients to "lead up," that is, to lead their direct supervisor. You can even lead outside of the workplace—within your family, your community, or your church. For the purpose of this book, we'll keep the term "leader" broad, yet focused in the context of the workplace.

LISTENING TO THE EXPERTS

What does it take to be an engaging leader?

"It takes a true leader to be totally unselfish, to see beyond the business metrics and the corporate pressures and put his or her people first. The most horrific waste in a company is the wasted minds and talents of people. When leaders do not recognize them, soon enough they will be surrounded by mediocrity. When I see the cost of developing an engaging culture from a monetary perspective, it is insignificant in relation to the tangible benefits it brings to the business. If I spend a dollar on creating engagement, the company gains a thousand back in results."

—Paolo Chiappina, Director
Lean and Global Process Sustainability

Engagement is present or lacking anytime a group of people comes together. In actuality, engagement starts with a single person…you. Are you engaged in your own life? Are you part of an engaged family, community, or church? Do you consider your work teams and workplace engaged? We can go on and on. Within the pages of this book our focus will remain on the work environment, but you can apply these principles across the landscape of your life.

This book is for anyone who wants to lead a cultural reformation or revolution within his or her work environment. Anyone who believes that it's no longer acceptable to spend years performing meaningless activity while secretly wishing he or she was retired and fishing. This book is for those who believe in a workplace where people are alive, using their talents, inspired, having fun, fulfilled, and valuing each other and their results.

This book is for those who are willing to take a stand and do something about the disengagement epidemic. People are ready to follow leaders who have the courage to speak passionately about these obstacles and be committed to reengage their people. *Are you that type of leader?*

Disengagement is the problem, and the solution is both obvious and difficult: *reengage our workforce.* In a *Business Week* advice column, former GE Chairman and CEO Jack Welch was asked which measurement gives the best sense of a company's health. He replied, "Employee engage-

Engagement starts with a single person…you.

ment first. It goes without saying that no company, small or large, can win over the long run without energized employees who believe in the mission and understand how to achieve it."[5] Trust your instincts, and let's partner up to do something about this issue.

Things to Consider

❖ Resist the temptation to overcomplicate this issue. Reengagement is simply the result of consistently applying the fundamental principles outlined in this book. Just because a highly engaged workplace is rare doesn't mean it's complicated.

❖ Step into the community of reformers. You're not in this alone. This book will guide and encourage you. I am on your side. The reformation has already started; join those who are making a difference now.

❖ Conduct a "gut check." Is this really important to you? Are you willing to stand up for those you lead? Does the thought of creating and fostering an engaging culture excite you? Scare you? Evoke some emotion in you? If you answer yes, let's continue. If not, reconsider.

CHAPTER TWO

Dig Down

Success depends upon previous preparation, and with-out such preparation, there is sure to be failure.
                                                    – Confucius

Entering the summer of 1982, I was eighteen years old and a recent high school graduate. My parents were wondering how I was going to earn funds toward my college tuition. I was wondering how I was going to make spending money, stay in shape, and get a great tan. Fortunately I didn't have to look any further than my girlfriend's dad, who owned his own construction company. This allowed me to skip the resume and interview process while moving directly to a superior hourly wage and lathering on the Hawaiian Tropic.

As a laborer for the John Bosco Construction Company, my job was hot, sweaty, and not exactly intellectually stimulating. We poured concrete footings and slabs. One of our jobs was to pour footings for cranes that unload huge container ships at Elizabeth Seaport, New Jersey. In all the manual labor, I learned some important lessons from the array of interesting professionals I worked beside.

Here's one thing I learned from the concrete construction industry: if you want to build a structure that is tall, stable, and strong, begin by digging down deep. This is not complex stuff. Engineers know that there's a direct relationship between building "up" and digging "down."

Footings and foundations are not the places to reduce costs. Even though the footings and foundation of a building aren't visible after construction is complete, wise builders don't cut corners here. Those who do try to save a few bucks on this phase of construction reap drastic consequences. Future winds or shifting earth can bring that building crashing down. Its gleaming exterior and architectural beauty won't help it stand strong if the proper foundation hasn't been laid.

That's where you start building your engaging culture—by digging down. In today's business climate it's tempting to begin building up right away, focusing on things that grab people's attention. It's exciting to lead projects that involve fancy, shiny stuff like a revised company logo and branding strategy, new Internet site, global sales presence, or the booth at the national trade show. That's all well and good. But the reality is, if you haven't dug your footings and foundation of engagement deep enough, all that can come crashing down very quickly. Those are the exact results many companies have experienced these past years through the "storms" of a particularly challenging economy.

Engaging the Soul

Digging down begins by understanding what engagement really is. The dictionary definition of engagement is "a binding, pledging, or coming together. A mutual pact, contract, or agreement."[6] I prefer to use a variation of John Fleming and Jim Asplund's definition from their book *Human Sigma*:

LISTENING TO THE EXPERTS

What does an engaging culture look like?

"Engagement is an environment where employees see the big picture. Where employees aspire to personal and professional development that is unique and customized to their needs. It's where employees act without direction because they know what is right. That, to me, is an engaging culture."

—Larry Diana, Owner
Express Employment Professionals

"Engagement means to give to people and serve them unconditionally. This has been the key to creating loyal friendships, creating trust, and attracting people to our vision. I never verbalized this until lately, but I've learned that giving is why people have followed me with respect."

—Paolo Chiappina, Director
Lean and Global Process Sustainability

"I think an engaging culture means that everybody is on board. Your whole team knows what your mission is. Everybody cares, everybody knows that what they do is important, and that their individual contribution to this organization makes a difference in our success."

— Mary Cloninger, CMPE, Executive Director
Carolina Neurosurgery & Spine Associates

"Engagement means that all my 'players' are in and aware of what's expected. It means being passionate believers in our work. It's bringing personal creativity, improv, and good judgment. This is unusual in dentistry, where the culture is typically oriented upon process and procedure. People are rarely rewarded or recognized for soft skills or relationship building. But in our practice, engagement means we want to spoil our patients and lavish them with care. To get that, I spoil my staff. I recently flew the entire office to Las Vegas for a conference. Our trip included limo rides, succulent dinners, a red rose, and a wonderful show. Never once did I ruin the experience by bringing up, 'Do you realize how much this cost?' I lavish them first so they will lavish our patients."

—Mark Hyman, DDS

Engagement is the ability to capture people's souls, hearts, and minds, instilling an intrinsic passion for action and excellence.[7]

Did you get that? Soul. Heart. Mind. That's where we are going to launch. What does that mean in the context of the workplace? It means engaging the entire person. Those who follow you are not one-dimensional line items on a profit and loss statement under the heading "payroll expense." You

❖ ❖ ❖

Those who work under your oversight seek an answer to their "why" question.

❖ ❖ ❖

lead three-dimensional beings. It will require courage to pursue the needs and confront the questions hidden in the souls, hearts, and minds of those who follow you.

Let's start by digging the footings for the soul. Your soul longs to reveal *purpose*—for it is there that purpose resides. The soul urges you to ask the question, *Why?* Those who work within your company or under your oversight seek an answer to their "why" question. It's a deep question, part of our human identity. *Why am I here? Why do I perform my work? Why is my work important? Why does my organization, department, or team exist?* When you understand the "why" of your work, you understand the purpose of your work. That's your design, and without it, you can expect to flounder.

As a leader, you can help others find the purpose their soul is seeking. When they ask and then answer the "why" question deep in their souls, they live and work with *conviction*. They gain understanding into how their work and purpose intertwine. They are no longer wandering aimlessly—they work with meaning and intention. And you can help them find this.

Think about great accomplishments in history. World War II was not won simply because of a well-designed strategy. People don't give their lives for strategy; people sacrifice for meaningful purpose that speaks to their souls, like fighting to defend the free world.

Dwight D. Eisenhower wrote a letter that spoke to the souls of soldiers headed into the fiercest battle ever fought. In his D-Day message to the troops, General Eisenhower lifted the morale of the men and women who made the largest invasion in history a success. His letter was addressed to the soldiers, sailors, and airmen of the Allied Expeditionary Force:

> You are about to embark upon the Great Crusade, toward which we have striven these many months. The eyes of the world are upon you. The hope and prayers of liberty-loving people everywhere march with you. In company with our brave allies and brothers-in-arms on other fronts, you will bring about the destruction of the German war machine, the elimination of Nazi tyranny over the oppressed peoples of Europe, and security for ourselves in a free world.

Without this compelling address, the outcome of the war could have been drastically different. Eisenhower called for nothing less than total and complete victory…and he got it. For all who read and heard it that fateful day, Eisenhower's message answered their soul's question—*Why?* Their purpose was to come to the aid of an oppressed people and secure the free world. For our fighting men and women, Dwight D. Eisenhower's words spoke to their souls. It led to conviction, and the rest is history.

Paolo Chiappina, Director of Lean and Global Process Sustainability, leads a small, powerful team that has achieved over $50 million in cost savings/avoidance for their organization over the past two years. One reason his team members accomplish such impressive results is that they get the answer to their why question. Paolo's band of champions understand why they exist and why they do their challenging work: they're creating a movement within their company and shifting a corporate culture.

This awareness fuels them as they travel around the globe, pouring knowledge and courage into their growing base of followers. Because Paolo has taken the necessary time to dig the purpose foundation for his team, they are committed and fiercely loyal to him and the cause they represent. Their conviction to their "why" is demonstrated in their day-to-day activity and the results they garner.

How does Paolo accomplish this? He invites his team into the "why" conversation. He listens. He has the courage to step away from the daily grind and discuss the team's purpose. He recognizes that his team members need conviction that originates from their souls, or their chances of surviving in such a challenging business climate would be diminished. He's an engaging leader.

Speaking to the Heart

Next, dig into the hearts of your followers. The heart's desire is to create *vision*. Vision is a future ideal state. The question that calls forth vision from your heart is, *What? What role will I play? What will things be like? What can we create? What will be different?* When we ask and answer the "what" question, vision is birthed.

"What role will I play? What will things be like? What can we create? What will be different?"

Hearts yearn to embrace vision. And the result of gaining this kind of clarity in your heart question is *inspiration*.

The journey of vision begins by becoming crystal clear on two key coordinates. First, describe with brutal honesty where you are now—your current state. It never surprises me how difficult it is for people and organizations to clearly and candidly express how things currently are. For most of my life, I lived in a "current state of denial." This is the condition of not being real about what is going on inside and around us. Before your heart casts great vision, first get real and honest about your present reality.

The next step is to determine where you want to be—your future ideal state. Your vision is most powerful when described in detail. Speak it. Write it down. Tell it like a story. What is happening in this future reality? Who is there? What is being accomplished? What sights, sounds, and smells can you imagine? What does it feel like for you to be there? The more specific you get, the more it speaks to your heart and the greater your inspiration.

Martin Luther King didn't gather throngs of followers because their hearts ached for a strategic plan or stretch goals. He didn't inspire by using charts and graphs. He simply had a dream that, when shared with others, provided a vision of what this country could be like, of what could be better and different for their children. He cast a vision for creating a future ideal state, and his dream altered the course of an entire country.

Engaging the Mind

Lastly, the minds of your followers must be engaged. The mind naturally seeks *goals*. Goals are critical for the logical portion of your being. They're essential for being held accountable to specific and measurable outcomes. Goals give your mind something concrete and tangible to grasp.

The question your mind is asking is, *How? How will I accomplish this? How will I get all this done in time? How will I get to my future desired state?* When you answer the "how" question, you gain goals and initiatives. These are necessary components to ensuring your purpose and vision can be accomplished. The result of engaging the "how" dialogue is *action* that propels you toward living out your purpose and vision, ensuring their achievement.

A word of caution: Historically, American organizations have overdone the mind-goals-how component. This is where most companies get entrenched—goals. The outcome of spending too much energy and focus here is a lack of conviction and inspiration, and this leads to meaningless goal-setting exercises and action steps that result in lackluster performance. Goals can feel like a safe place from which to lead. By remaining in the mind-goals-how position, you feel protected from the dangers of entering the hearts and souls of yourself and others. Beware: This is not for you! Act courageously and venture into the risky venues of heart and soul.

Here's a summary of how this foundation looks:

Soul→longs for **Purpose**→asks the question **Why?**
→leads to **Conviction**
Heart→desires **Vision**→asks the question **What?**
→leads to **Inspiration**
Mind→seeks **Goals**→asks the question **How?**
→leads to **Action**

What would be different if you were surrounded by people whose souls, hearts, and minds were passionately engaged in meaningful work? What might that mean to your success?

In 2006, The Conference Board, a nonprofit business membership and research organization, published an article called "Employee Engagement: A Review of Current Research and Its Implications."[8] It determined that the following qualities exist in an engaging culture. On a scale of 1 (lowest score) to 10 (highest score) how would you rate your organization or team in these areas?

___ **Trust and integrity.** People are congruent and authentic, not perfect. There are plenty of agendas, none of them hidden.

___ **Purpose.** People view their work as meaningful and stimulating.

___ **Big-picture perspective.** Employees understand how their work contributes to the company's success and performance.

___ **Opportunity.** The avenues for individual growth and development are clear. The organization makes an effort to provide tools and support for employees' improvement.

___ **Ownership.** People demonstrate a pride in their company/organization.

___ **Community.** Strong relationships exist among coworkers/team members and with their managers.

There's plenty at stake here besides the obvious issues of employee productivity and corporate profits. Trust. Loyalty.

Meaningful work. Creativity. Innovation. Strong relationships. Customer service. Energy. Excitement. Fun. All of these qualities hinge on whether or not people are functioning within engaging environments.

Pouring concrete during my summer breaks was tough and dirty work. I was often the guy who climbed down into the footings and foundations to ensure they were ready to pour. In fact, this work caused me to repeat over and over again in my mind, *This is why I'm going to college. This is why I'm going to college.* Yet despite the dirt and labor, it was important work that had great impact on the stability and strength of the cranes and buildings that rose up from our well-laid foundations. So it is with leaders who aspire to create and foster engaging cultures. This too can be tough and dirty work. It may take years before the fruit of your labor is fully visible and recognized. This is more of a calling than a job description, so if you feel the conviction deep down in your soul to lead in this manner—let's dig, baby. Let's start digging.

Fundamental Principles + Application = Results

After you've poured the footings and laid the foundation of soul, heart, and mind, you're ready to begin building your culture "up." This is done with the most enduring materials you can find: fundamental principles. Life has repeatedly taught me to believe in fundamentals.

I'm here to tell you that if you want a life that is engaging, focus on the fundamentals.

Fundamental principles aren't very exciting or glamorous, so they don't get much press. I'm here to tell you that if you want a life that is engaging, focus on the fundamentals. Let's discuss three reasons fundamentals work.

First, fundamentals avail themselves to everyone. They are nondiscriminatory. No special skills or advanced degrees are needed. They are inclusive, not exclusive. Michael Jordan could fly on the basketball court; God instilled that special ability in him. You've seen him jump from the free throw line, soar like an eagle, tongue out, and gracefully slam the basketball through the hoop. This talent is not a fundamental; it's a gift that is rarely inclusive to the rest of us.

Pictures of Michael flying through the air have been plastered on sports posters and highlight films...but it never earned him a championship. When head coach Phil Jackson appeared in Michael's life with the Chicago Bulls, he insisted on the execution of fundamental basketball principles (read *Mindgames: Phil Jackson's Long Strange Journey*). These are the same basketball fundamentals that children practice in summer camp without agents or multimillion-dollar endorsement deals.

Jackson surrounded Michael with a team that would do the same. Multiple championships followed. You may not be able to fly through the air and slam-dunk, but you can execute a fundamentally sound two-handed chest pass. No, you won't wind up in the highlight films, but you could hold up your own personal "championship" trophy of success.

Second, fundamentals are timeless. No need to reinvent, rename, or reengineer a fundamental. The Bible says that there is nothing new under the sun. Fundamental principles have worked, do work, and will work. It doesn't matter how many generations you have employed in your workplace. Certain fundamentals are important to people from eighteen to eighty years old. It's not the principles that are being tested; you are being tested. Are you willing to learn from the past and make

An engaging leader already lives within you. It's waiting to manifest through you and as you.

application within your life today so that in the future, things will be different and better?

Third, fundamentals get results. Things happen. This is not fluff. If you apply these principles to your life, things will change. You will change. Scary thought? Yes, but the only scarier thought is no change. The idea that I might not develop, not grow, or not fulfill my ultimate calling scares me more than the fear of change.

Remember the saying, "Knowledge is power?" It's a lie. Back in the day when information was the domain of a privileged few, this made sense. Now it's simply a mouse-click away for anyone. Knowledge is no longer power. Application is the new power. Author and speaker Mark Sanborn said, "The difference between excellence and mediocrity is the difference between common knowledge and consistent application."[9] All of the principles shared in this book are fundamental. You already know them. You may or may not be applying them. That's the difference between engaging leaders and mediocre ones: *application*.

Because of this, it's unrealistic to expect lasting change to occur from reading a book, attending a seminar, or listening to CDs in your car. Growth and change come from taking what you *know* and transferring it into what you *do*. The eighteenth-century German scientist and writer Johann Wolfgang von Goethe said, "Knowing is not enough; we must apply. Willing is not enough; we must do."[10] No one and nothing changes without application—got it?

In chapter three, we will begin unpacking nine fundamental principles that, when diligently applied, will transform you into an engaging leader. I rediscovered these age-old values through a number of means. I've taken an open and honest look at my own successes and shortcomings as a life-long leader. I have paid close attention to what does and doesn't work for the leaders I have the privilege to call my clients. I've scoured the literature and research regarding effective leadership.

You can have a successful journey of creating and fostering an engaging workplace. Are you ready to dig down and capture the souls, hearts, and minds of your people? Are you willing to apply a few fundamental principles? If so, then you're set to lead the change and build a strong, stable, and meaningful culture. You don't have to lose 'em—you can engage 'em. Let's get to work!

Namaste

I first learned of the word *Namaste* a few years ago while listening to one of my spiritual teachers. It is a common spoken greeting or salutation on the Indian subcontinent. It has several meanings, one of which is, "I respect the divinity in you that is also within me." Beautiful. Meaningful. It acknowledges the greatness and abilities that already reside in each of us.

An engaging leader already lives within you. It's waiting to manifest through and as you. Like the acorn seed encapsulates the mighty oak tree, you hold within yourself the essence of an emerging, engaging leader. Don't go searching for what you already possess. You are not lacking. You are amazingly capable.

This book is a reminder of who you already are. All that is needed is your practice—*the outward expression of your inner being*. Practice. Apply these principles and observe with awe and wonder as the "mighty oak" of you emerges and unfolds into an engaging leader who changes the global workplace, one culture at a time—your culture. I respect the engaging leader in you that is also within me. *Namaste.*

Recommended Action Steps

❖ Commit to paying attention to your culture. Begin to intently observe and listen to those whom you lead. What do you see? What do you hear? What do you feel? The idea here is to become a student of your culture and begin to see things the way your followers see them. Record your honest findings.

❖ Review your company or team's mission/vision statement. Does it speak to the souls, hearts, and minds of those whom you lead? Does it uncover purpose, vision, and goals? Does it answer the questions *why?*, *what?*, and *how?* Does it generate conviction, inspiration, and action? Be honest with yourself. Ask others their opinion. If it needs work, partner with your team to revamp it until your answers become "Yes!"

❖ Make a list with two columns. One heading should read: *What I am willing to do to fulfill my calling as an engaging leader.* The second heading should read: *What I am not willing to do to fulfill my calling as an engaging leader.* Observe your answers. What does this say about your willingness and readiness to move forward?

CHAPTER THREE

Lead Thyself

*You are an original, an utterly unique human being.
You cannot have the life you want, make the decisions
you want, or be the leader you are capable of being
until your actions represent an authentic expression of
who you really are, or who you wish to become.*
—Susan Scott, *Fierce Conversations*

The alarm rang shrilly as the clock read 4:00 a.m. My arm
flinched involuntarily as it levered over to hit the button and
turn it off. The murkiness of my sleep world slowly faded as the
dim contours of my bedroom came into focus, and I staggered
groggily into the bathroom. I flipped on the light and looked
at the bleary face in the mirror. With a twinge of betrayal, I
exclaimed angrily, "I thought I fired you yesterday. The nerve of
you to show up here in my bathroom!" This is the frustration I
feel at my sometimes futile attempts to lead myself.

Lead Thyself is your first fundamental principle...and
for good reason. Frankly, it's the toughest. Embracing your
authentic self and taking responsibility for who and where
you are is so challenging that it causes many a person to turn
back. Yet without the courage and humility to uncover who
you really are and cease making excuses, you cannot earn
the right to lead others in an engaging manner. It's tricky to
lead where you have not been and impossible to give what
you have not received.

Let's begin with you. You deserve it. Those you lead need to sense that you have traveled this path of self-leadership, that you have faced—and conquered—that image in the mirror each morning.

Perhaps the seventies rock group the Who sang it best:

Well, who are you? (Who are you? Who, who, who, who?)
I really wanna know (Who are you? Who, who, who, who?)
Tell me, who are you? (Who are you? Who, who, who, who?)
'Cause I really wanna know (Who are you? Who, who, who, who?)[11]

The Path to Yourself

When my daughter Taylor was seven, she was terrified of storms. Particularly, the ones that suddenly appear during late summer afternoons: dark clouds quickly approaching, treetops whipping in the wind, rain coming down sideways. She would retreat to the living room couch, lie in the fetal position, and shake violently. This didn't sit well with me. I'm her dad. Dads fix things, and this needed to be fixed.

During one of these storms, I approached her trembling body, sure that I could conquer this challenge. I said, "Taylor, I am your dad. I will protect you. This storm will not harm you as long as I am here." In spite of my comforting words, she continued to shake and be afraid.

Then came another summer storm. I approached the couch with a more logical thought this time, "Taylor, we live in central North Carolina," I said. "The weather patterns here are rarely disastrous. We are safe from floods, tornadoes,

❋ ❋ ❋

"Dad, what are you afraid of?"

❋ ❋ ❋

and usually hurricanes. This storm will pass; you are safe." She continued to tremble. Again, my words failed to make an impact. A few weeks later another storm rolled in, and I had an idea. "Taylor, our house was built in the 1940s. Back then, two-by-fours were actually two inches high and four inches wide; now they are smaller. This house is sturdy and strong. You are safe here; the storm will pass, and you will be fine." But the trembling did not stop. Strike three. This was not the result I was expecting, and I was frustrated with my lack of success.

A short time later, after receiving some heart-felt advice from a friend, I decided to try yet a different tactic. As the next summer storm zeroed in on our neighborhood, I found Taylor in her usual spot, trembling on the living room couch. I sat down beside her, put my hand on her shoulder, and said, "Taylor, it's okay to be afraid."

She glanced up at me with her youthful eyes and asked, "Dad, what are you afraid of?" *Crap! My friend never told me about this part. Think fast,* I thought to myself. *If I were to tell her the truth, I'd have to say that, like most men, I'm afraid of having to talk about what I'm afraid of. No, no, I can't tell her that.* So, in that instant, I spoke from my heart.

"I guess I'm most afraid of losing you or your sister." She sat up, and we began a conversation. The trembling stopped. Just like that, things changed.

As I reflect back on that event, here's what I learned. I thought my daughter needed a superhero dad, a meteorologist dad, or perhaps an engineer dad. I felt certain that one of those images would make her feel safe. Yet all along, she was searching for just two things—the freedom to be herself and the opportunity to know her real dad, her authentic dad. A dad who can admit that sometimes he's afraid and doesn't always know the answers. In that moment I chose to lead authentically, and my daughter willingly followed. She was engaged by my openness.

LISTENING TO THE EXPERTS

What has helped you create an engaging workplace?

"First, I had to get clear on the personal side about what really defines me—who I am—and there are five words I came up with to describe myself. These values play out in my personal life, my volunteer efforts, and my work efforts: I exist to be creative, playful, inspiring, passionate, and to make a difference. So anything that contributes to those five values, I'm all over it. Then I have to prioritize how I spend my time. I've got to take time for myself, my family, for Todd Herman Associates, and then volunteer activities—Greensboro Urban Ministry, First Lutheran Church, and the Boy Scouts. But just recognizing those five personal values has been key in crafting an engaging workplace. Being engaged is really the only option if you come to work with me.

Having an engaged workforce that really enjoys what they do is special. I've had people leave the firm and then tell me, 'You've got the best workplace I've ever been in.' My current employees tell me that, too; maybe they're just sucking up to me, but I don't think so."

—Todd Herman, CPS, CITP, President
Todd Herman & Associates PA

Katherine Sharp says it like this, "Sometime in your life, you will go on a journey. It will be the longest journey you have ever taken. It is the journey to find yourself."[12] So it is with engaging leaders. You must have the courage to travel the path to yourself. In other words, *lead thyself* first.

Remove the Wax

Our word *sincere* comes from two Latin words—*sine* ("without") and *cera* ("wax"). A theory is that in Roman times, local craftsmen would apply colored wax on sculptures or pottery to hide their defects and imperfections. Ultimately, with use or exposure to the elements, the wax would wear off and the natural flaws or manmade mistakes within the artwork would again become visible. Some artisans with higher standards would place a sign over their workshops to advertise their craft as *sine cera*. The message they were sending was that their works of art were without wax, the real deal, not covered by an illusion—they were authentic.

Engaging individuals are *sine cera*—imperfect works of art. Yet more often than not, we encounter leaders who are wearing a "mask," our modern terminology for "wax." It's a way of hiding or covering up weaknesses, flaws, scars, and natural imperfections. It's a way of pretending to be something you aren't. Perhaps you wish to appear strong or flawless. Whether you're wearing a mask or covered up with wax, the results are the same: in an attempt to appear different than you really are, a disconnect develops between yourself and others. Actually, a disconnect develops within yourself.

Leaders who build engaging cultures do so first and foremost by discovering, embracing, and utilizing their own unique talents and strengths while acknowledging and accepting their imperfections. They become genuine, authentic, and approachable. They become comfortable with themselves. They are real.

I often work with leaders and speakers who try to become someone they think others want them to be. Yet in reality, people simply crave a genuine, authentic, real, wax-free leader. By leading with sincerity, you give others permission to be authentic themselves. They are attracted by your courage and willingness to lay down your mask and remove the built-up wax. People long to be authentic, and you can model this for them. You can help them find the courage to take their own journey to find themselves. They will follow your example.

In his book *Leading With A Limp*, Dan Allender writes:

> The truth about confession is that it doesn't lead to people's weakness and disrespect; instead, it transforms the leader's character and earns her greater respect and power. This is the strange paradox of leading: to the degree you attempt to hide or dissemble your weaknesses, the more you will need to control those you lead, the more insecure you will become, and the more rigidity you will impose—prompting the ultimate departure of your best people.[13]

Often times, our need to pretend and cover up stems from a belief that we are not enough, that on our own we are lacking. I remember the line from a song by the band America: "No, Oz never did give nothin' to the Tin Man that he didn't, didn't already have."[14] In *The Wizard of Oz*, Dorothy portrayed an engaging leader. She was *sine cera*. She didn't have to "be" anything more than she was. She had the ability to see the distinctive traits residing with others and within herself.

LISTENING TO THE EXPERTS

What has helped you create an engaging workplace?

"I want to give my employees an opportunity to see the big picture. And to do that, I share a lot of information about the company with them: We do a monthly review and go through the financials, we go through the trends. Are sales up, down, even? Are gross profits up or down? Are we cash-flow positive, did we have a hiccup during the month? The employees are privy to all this information. When things are going great, we're all high-fiving; if they're not, we don't feel threatened because we know this is a temporary thing, and we all pull together. They don't look at it and think, 'Oh my goodness, am I going to lose my job?' They look at it and say, "Okay, we've got to really bear down; we've got to really focus this month.' That's what I call 'big picture.' I share the business with them as though they were partners.

"It all starts with me. If I'm not willing to be transparent and share information with my team and trust that they'll handle that information well, then how can I be trusted? Trust is fundamental in any business. If you don't have it, then you'll have people making excuses and giving alibis. They'll avoid creative and constructive things for the good of the business because they'll never know when a comment could be used against them. They'll never know when the boss is withholding information and how that is going to affect them. So I put my cards on the table and take that part out of the equation.

> "'Transparency' is a key word in my management style. If I make a mistake, the first thing I do in a meeting is say, 'You know, I've made a mistake.' I'll admit it and apologize. 'I didn't use good judgment.' They're ready to move the building for me when I do that."
>
> —Larry Diana, Owner
> Express Employment Professionals

Without first knowing herself, she would have been unable to effectively recognize and call upon the unique talents and gifts of her "team." As a result, the Scarecrow would still be stuck on a stick, the Lion cowering behind his fears, and the Tin Man still frozen emotionless. Instead, they bonded together, overcame adversity, supported each other, and ultimately accomplished some pretty important outcomes: a brain, some courage, a heart, and a way home. That's an engaged "culture" on a meaningful journey together.

Fear and Wax

The Book of Lists conducted a survey to determine the greatest fears among Americans. Speaking before a group is number one. Death is number seven. Apparently, if you're an American and headed to a funeral, you would choose the casket over the eulogy. The facts are clear—public speaking is scary!

I do a lot of work helping people become more powerful and engaging presenters. My teaching methods are nontraditional: Most people expect to be told what to do and what not to do in order to improve their presentation skills.

But this can lead to a mechanical and unnatural presentation style, which heightens the biggest challenge facing presenters—fear of being themselves.

I am convinced that everyone has the ability to speak effectively. Everyone has something to share. Everyone has unique insights and experiences that can inspire an audience. Yet so many leaders and presenters feel inadequate just being themselves. Fear loves wax.

The single most destructive thought in the mind of presenters during the walk from their seat to the stage is this: *I'm not enough. In order for this audience to accept me, I must pretend to be someone else.* In that moment, your most powerful presentation tool—your own authenticity—is lost. Truth be told, the audience is eager to know you. Giving them insight into who you really are creates a bond. Audiences crave hearing someone who has the courage to be real. You are more than enough. Successful speakers, like successful leaders, recognize the unique qualities they possess and utilize them in their presentation.

One time I worked with a vice president of operations for a local manufacturing company. The material he presented was often dry, and he was having a hard time capturing and keeping the attention of his audience. After listening to a couple of his presentations, it became clear that his material was indeed dry and, yes, boring.

Your most powerful position in anything you do comes from the willingness to be your true self.

I asked him what he liked to do in his free time, what type of activities he did with his children, what he did to unwind. After some conversation, he told me he played the harmonica in a blues band. *Eureka!* I had him describe for me how he behaved when on stage with his band. He said he normally wore shades, a cool hat, and kept his body moving to the rhythm of the songs. We agreed that this was a natural and comfortable way for him to react when he was on the stage playing jazz or the blues.

I then asked, "Where is that person Monday through Friday? Where is that person when you have a presentation to make?" By the time our collaboration had ended, he had used his harmonica in a presentation (about profit margins) and had the entire audience on their feet singing a blues song. Instead of acting like he thought he was supposed to (boring), he decided to be himself. He gained the courage to trust his own authenticity, and the results were astounding.

Your most powerful position in anything you do comes from the willingness to be your true self. It is imperative that you have the courage to lead in that way, and it is impossible to engage a person or a group for very long when you are pretending. That house of cards will collapse.

I can recall a morning, years ago, when I hurried into my company. I heard a cheerful, "Good morning, Rich! How ya doing today?" Without thinking (historically, that has gotten me into trouble), I briefly glanced at Dawn and said, "Great. And if I wasn't, I wouldn't let you know anyway."

I continued walking at a quick enough pace to maintain my target heart rate, feeling confidently smug with my response. Now I look back and cringe. What a joke. The phrase, "I wouldn't let you know anyway" was code, meaning, "I'm a fake, and I don't have the courage or honesty to tell you the truth." What a poser. Because I lacked self-confidence and self-awareness, I was forced to keep people at a distance and use "wax" to cover up who I really was. That kept me from building honest relationships and being an effective leader. And it hindered me from truly engaging my team.

I've heard it said that we can impress from afar but only impact from up close. I have spent years trying hard to appear impressive; not only was it exhausting, but the results were less than desirable. I decided to change—to face the fear of removing my masks and wax. It wasn't always easy, yet I've never regretted it.

Born To Run

I grew up in Freehold, New Jersey, a town near the shore and famous for producing Bruce Springsteen. I vividly recall my senior year of high school: how anxious I was to leave my home state, ready to run from the cold, the overcast skies, the crowding, my friends, and all that was holding me back. I was running toward a fresh start, headed toward new dreams. My route would take me five hundred miles south to the University of North Carolina at Greensboro. My dreams included winning national championships and playing professional soccer. I could see it so clearly. I would return to Jersey a hero—the kid who left, chased down his dreams, and returned on top of the world. I was prepared to compete, complete with a blue-collar work ethic and a high tolerance for pain.

As I reflect back, it seems like I was running practically half my life. After graduating from UNCG (national championships, three; professional soccer career, none), the race continued with the need to appear successful in business, family, church, and everywhere else. There was an incessant need to look good and have the right stuff. Yet somewhere in my late thirties to early forties, all the pretending began to wear on me. Not just physically, but emotionally and spiritually as well.

At some point I decided to stop running and be still, to halt the blurring motion of movement and take a look inside of myself—and perhaps gain the insight and wisdom Ms. Teague was speaking of. What I discovered was significant: I had not been running from New Jersey, overcast skies, crowded places, or my friends. I was running from the emptiness, from the confusion, and from the conflict that resided within me. I was not running to national championships or professional soccer; I was running toward the hope that personal accomplishments would prove I was valuable, important, and significant after all. Without even knowing it, I was attempting to find peace…on the wrong course. I have since learned that the real race is never outside myself; it's always inside of me.

Things are different now. I'm still running—typically 10Ks and half-marathons. More than that, I am discovering peace. I am finding myself. It's hard to believe that it would take this long to get to know who I am when I've been here all along. It has, at times, been an exhausting and exhilarating journey, and I believe it was meant to be that way. Instead of running from myself, I now run toward the person I'm meant to be. My life course is purposeful and meaningful.

❖ ❖ ❖

My strengths, as well as my weaknesses, flaws, scars, and imperfections have all shaped who I am. It's all part of my humanity.

❖ ❖ ❖

In his book *Wild at Heart*, John Eldredge says that both boys and men, deep in their hearts, are seeking an answer to the same question: *do I have what it takes?* My race has led to my own answer: yes. I lack nothing. What I've been seeking has been here all along. It just took time, courage, and insight to discover it.

Life has dealt me some challenges. How about you? I've experienced the death of my mom from lung cancer, being fired from a company I once owned, a divorce, the death of my second wife due to breast cancer, and plenty of time spent in counseling. This is part of who I am, part of my road to now. And I know that through challenging times, I have refined the traits and qualities that make me successful. These life situations have allowed me to be more compassionate with others, to grow in my faith, to slow my pace of life, to rethink my priorities, and to become more committed to causes that move me. My strengths, as well as my weaknesses, flaws, scars, and imperfections have all shaped who I am. It's all part of my realness—my humanity.

Iyanla Vanzant wrote, "If you can admit you are afraid and keep moving, you will be released from the fear."[15] You are not alone in your fear of removing your wax. Be courageous. Admit it and remove it. You won't regret it.

Remember Joey from Jersey? Some time ago, he called with tickets to a Bruce Springsteen concert. Our reunion to the music of the Boss was like a homecoming. It doesn't get much better than that. Toward the end of the two-hour concert, thousands in the audience were standing, swaying, and belting out a line from Bruce's 1975 hit, "Tramps like us, baby, we were born to run."[16]

Take Responsibility

After you are willing to embrace your own authenticity and "get real" with yourself, you'll be ready to face the challenges of reengagement. Here's your next step: take 100 percent responsibility. This begins by asking yourself tough questions: *What is my role in this? How might I be contributing to disengagement?* This is where leaders start to earn respect—by asking the questions that others run from. It takes no skill or courage to think, *This is not my fault. I'm the reason these people have a job. I've taken huge risks so they can feed their families. In these tough economic times they should be thanking me for their paycheck.*

Nice try.

Feeling that way is understandable, but it's not what is needed. It is much more effective to begin recognizing your own role in creating a culture that has not always been an ideal, engaging environment. Instead of asking, *How in the world did I end up in this mess?* try, *What is the meaning of the mess I am in?* When I began working with one of my clients, Tony Johnson, he did just that, immediately earning my respect. He started our consulting relationship by stating, "Rich, we're in this place because I've allowed it to happen. I take full responsibility for where my company is, and I know we need to change. I'll do whatever it takes to initiate change."

Tony worked hard for over a year to rebuild strong relationships with his key managers, to create a clear and compelling vision for his company, and to earn their intellectual and emotion belief in his leadership. It's that simple. It's that difficult. It's uncommon.

Now is not the time to play the victim card. Now is not the time for whining. Try taking a proactive approach to personal responsibility by asking questions like, *How can I help create an engaging culture? What can I do to help solve this problem? How can I move this vision forward?*

Taking 100 percent responsibility has nothing to do with blame. You're not blaming yourself or others. Blame comes from a place of lack, limitation, and scarcity. Taking responsibility emerges from opportunity, plenty, and abundance. Taking responsibility for your role in any life experience is freeing. It frees you up to move ahead and create new and more effective results.

Change begins with you. Not *them* or even *us*. Teams don't change. Departments and organizations don't change. "They" don't change. People change…one at a time! A culture shift is nothing more than people who represent that culture changing individually. And the only place you can begin change is with yourself. By acting on this decision, you can launch the change necessary to impact your culture. It starts with you. So if you're ready, let's learn how to make it personal in the next chapter.

Recommended Action Steps

❖ Get quiet. Carve out time for silence in your life. Think. This is the first step in embracing your authenticity. This can be uncomfortable at first if you're not used to being still. Make a regular appointment with yourself to sit quietly and think.

❖ Write down your thoughts. Journaling is an important habit for engaging leaders. It's nothing more than recording thoughts, ideas, or feelings that come into your mind throughout the day. Spelling and grammar don't count. Just begin writing.

❖ Whenever you encounter a situation you wish could be better or different, ask yourself the following questions:

- What is my role in this? How am I contributing to this outcome?
- What needs to change in me?
- What do I need to help me grow in this area?
- What insight am I to gain from these circumstances?

CHAPTER FOUR

Let Them In

It is easy to be brave from a safe distance.

– Aesop

Do you recall that World War II poster of Uncle Sam? It read, "I Want You," and I could feel his finger pointed straight at me. It was a compelling poster because there's no mistaking who he's talking to. There's no question that Uncle Sam wants me because I can make a difference. He knows that each individual is key to making an impact on a local or global level. That's a powerful idea.

Here's the deal: Imagine that same poster. Only this time, the picture includes the faces of the people who look to you for leadership. That might be your team, direct reports, peers, family, community, or church. They all have their fingers pointing straight at you. Now, close your eyes...Can you see it? *They want you.* Yes, you. It's okay to admit it: they want you because you're their leader. You're important to them!

Bob Nelson, author of *1001 Ways to Reward Employees*, conducted a survey of fifteen hundred employees. He wanted to know in these tight, stressful, changing times what recognition items were most important to corporate workers. Number six was "time with their manager." Do you ever think of yourself as a top-ten recognition item? How does that feel? Here's how Nelson explains it:

In today's fast-paced world of work in which everyone is expected to get more done faster, personal time with one's manager is in itself also a form of recognition. As managers are busier, taking the time with employees is all the more important to do. As Roy Moody, president of Roy Moody Associates puts it: "The greatest motivational act one person can do for another is to listen."[17]

You might be wondering where money appeared in this survey. A "cash reward" ranked fifteenth. There you have it. When it comes to demonstrating how important you are, these results show you're more valuable than cash! I guess cash is not king (or queen)—you are. Now that you have connected with your authentic self in the last chapter, it's time to show the real you to those you lead. Dare to give them what they want: more of yourself. Your second fundamental principle is **Let Them In**.

For too many years leaders have focused on policies and procedures and ignored the importance of meaningful relationships. Howard Behar, who runs Starbucks' retail operations once said, "We are not in the coffee business, serving people. We are in the people business, serving coffee." He gets it. We are all in the relationship business.

Often I find that leaders and organizations get confused over the business they're really in. This confusion comes from thinking that their business is the same as their industry or products. They're not one and the same. You owe it to your customers and clients to be an expert within your industry and have cutting-edge, world-class products. But neither of these are your business. Your business is relationships, the ones that connect you with your people and customers.

The Gift of Presence

Once, while attending a homeschool conference, I heard a speaker address the age-old debate of "quality time versus quantity time." He concluded by telling us parents in the audience that "quality time magically appears somewhere in the midst of quantity time." That has stuck with me, and it makes sense at home as well as at work.

Spend a greater quantity of time with the people you lead and influence. Where are you going to find this time? You decide…but it must be done if you want loyalty.

One specific way to demonstrate your understanding of the relationship business is to spend a greater quantity of time with the people you lead and influence. Where are you going to find this time? How are you going to make the necessary moments available? You decide…but it must be done if you want the quality of relationships that produce commitment and loyalty.

It is important that you be fully present for the people you lead. Not just in the building, but available and accessible. Today, it's harder than ever to really "be where you are." The battle to be fully present is being lost on both personal and corporate fronts.

The challenge of being present became obvious to me one day when running in a local park. There's nothing that clears my head like running in the midst of nature; these times of solitude are when I get my best thinking done. I solve problems, create speeches, invent chapters for my books, and hear the voice of God. I often run past people in the park who are talking on their cell phones or have an iPod strapped to their bicep or some other technology device dangling from their waistline. I cringe. They are walking in a beautiful park, but they're not there. They are not present to their environment, but rather are allowing distractions to rob them of their present moment.

Staci Eldredge, author of *Captivating*, wrote, "The gift of presence is a rare and beautiful gift. To come—unguarded, undistracted—and be fully present, fully engaged with who-ever we are with at that moment."[18] When I typed in this quote, it was Mother's Day, and I couldn't help thinking that this is why mothers are loved and revered. They know how to give us the gift of their presence. Mothers are good leaders because they engage their "followers." Your followers desperately want to receive the gift of your presence. Will they get the chance?

Open Up

While watching the movie *Saving Private Ryan,* I became mesmerized by the relationships within the group of men that were sent to find Private James Francis Ryan. Their leader was Captain John H. Miller, played by Tom Hanks. While he was determined to keep his civilian life at a distance from his platoon, they ached to know more about him. Deep into their mission, to break up the tension and dissension between his men, he began to tell them stories about who he really was. He's not just a captain; he is a husband and schoolteacher with real dreams of returning home someday. His men are locked in on him as he shares these parts of himself. No one can engage whole-heartedly with the person who remains a mystery.

I've worked beside some inspiring leaders who have built engaging cultures. Tom Turner is one of them. I met with Tom and his six key managers over a year's span. Tom wanted to create ongoing learning opportunities that would help his team members grow personally and professionally. He was smart enough to know that better people make better organizations.

Tom didn't just "send" his team to workshops; he was fully involved with the entire process. When it came time for him to share his personal development vision, he let it all out. He shared with his team how he attempted to create and maintain balance in his own life, how he wanted to be a good dad, and why that was important to him. If that meant leaving work in time to coach his son's baseball team, he would do it.

Tom also shared his professional goals. He discussed where he wanted to "grow to" in the company and the skills he still needed to get there. He mentioned how important his team was to him and the type of leader he wanted to be for them. He shared how his hero, his own dad, had shaped him as a person and as a leader. Parts of Tom's personal and professional vision were so meaningful to him, they caused him to become emotional, but he didn't hold that back either.

This is what I know about the six people who follow Tom Turner: They are fiercely loyal to him. They are committed to their own personal development, to the department goals that they set together, and to their leader. They respect and admire him. You can see it in their eyes, hear it in their voice, and watch it in their actions. They are fully engaged—

souls, hearts, and minds. And this is because Tom is real; he lets them in. He doesn't put on the "corporate" face when he comes to work. He wears his own face consistently and is rid of wax. This posture takes courage and gets results.

LISTENING TO THE EXPERTS

How do you connect with your people?

"I think technology has helped us in a lot of ways but hurt us in others. We don't have time to connect with each other anymore. You know, we've got our Blackberrys when we're sitting at home, trying to talk to our spouses. We're still in a people business, and we've got to treat it as such. For us, it's a priority to connect with our employees, and we do that, even at the president level. I go one-on-one with my people, just like you and me now. We don't do that over e-mail. Old Dominion is still a family atmosphere. That's the reason we're still making a profit in this economy and most of our competitors aren't."

—Marty Freeman, Senior Vice President of Sales and National Accounts, Old Dominion Freight Line

"To create this sort of culture, you have to invest in people in a variety of ways. You can invest by providing education for them; you can invest by giving them ways to grow, personally and professionally. Maybe they want to move up in the organization, maybe not; maybe they are better at what they do and enjoy what they do. I think there are little things that go a long way:

> Every five years we give employees an anniversary gift. They know that their gift is coming. You buy their lunch periodically. They sound like little things, but they make people feel valued. Like on the day it snowed, people made it into work. They were complaining, but they made it in because they knew we had work to do. I ordered pizza and salad for everybody. It's just the little things that show that you care, that you value your people. I think those types of things help them engage. And it's a two-way street: as the employer, you have to be engaged in them, buy into what they're doing, and provide something for them as well."
>
> —Mary Cloninger, CMPE, Executive Director
> Carolina Neurosurgery & Spine Associates

Peeling Back the Myths

Tom, and other courageous leaders like him, has helped debunk some corporate myths. Let's address a few. One goes like this: "I don't bring my personal life to work." What does that mean? Can you actually live two separate lives? Exactly where on your soul, heart, or mind do you draw the line that splits your personal and professional self? You are not a one-dimensional being, and you cannot be a one-dimensional leader. To be an engaging leader, you must willingly share all of yourself with the people you lead. If you do not get personal, you will default to leading impersonally—and that doesn't work very well.

Let's consider another corporate myth: "I don't get too close to my people. That just leads to trouble, so I keep a safe distance." Since most of these comments come from men, I can attempt to interpret this primitive language for you: "I am afraid of getting close to people. I don't know myself that well, and I fear that if others get too close to me, they might see through my mask and discover I'm merely human!" Ken Lehman, cofounder of Winning Workplaces, a nonprofit that yearly anoints America's Top Small Company Workplaces, simply states, "If you are a good leader, then your people know you."[19] Enough already. Stop the lies.

A question I'm often asked is, "Rich, how about keeping appropriate boundaries? Doesn't a leader have to know where to draw the line?" Here's my response: We have a crisis in corporate America—the lack of meaningful relationships between leaders and followers. Let's not resist the solution because a minuscule percentage of people have abused it.

Have you seen news reports when a commercial airliner crashes? Have you continued to fly? Yes, because you know it remains the safest way to travel, even though every crash makes the headlines. Don't let a few highly publicized relationship abuses stop you from doing what is right and effective. Those who are looking to take advantage of others, who are clueless when it comes to understanding appropriate boundaries, aren't reading this book. You are. You can make the difference.

Ultimately, we choose to follow people we know, respect, and trust. If you have the title "Leader," "Supervisor," or "Manager" attached to your name, look behind you. Anyone following? If not, you're just out for a walk.

In one of the final moments of *Saving Private Ryan*, a mortally wounded Captain Miller pulls the rescued Ryan close and whispers in his ear, "Earn this…" Those words ring true today. There was a great cost that went into saving the life of Private Ryan. So it is with creating an engaging culture. You will pay a price—as an engaging leader, you will need to earn this. You build and foster an engaging culture by building strong, trusting relationships and by allowing others to get close to you. Share who you are. They want you—let them in.

Recommended Action Steps

❖ Begin to share with your team things about yourself that they might not know from working with you. Start slowly. Tell them about your family, your hobbies, your interests, where you grew up, and what and who has shaped your life. Have the courage to be a leader who discloses your true self.

❖ Reduce your multitasking. My brother, an elite-level track coach, said it best when I asked him about the benefits of cross training (the athletes' way of multitasking): "It's a sure way to become mediocre in several events." If you're mediocre at building meaningful relationships with those you lead, perhaps you should focus more attention and time on them.

❖ Look at your calendar and ask, "What actions have I taken this week and what commitments do I have scheduled that are focused on strengthening strategic relationships in my work and life?" Hold yourself accountable for aligning what you do with what you believe. Make time for letting people have what they want: You.

CHAPTER FIVE

Make It Personal

It doesn't take a hero to order men into battle. It takes a
hero to be one of those men who goes into battle.
— General Norman Schwarzkopf

On a chilly January afternoon when my daughter Carley was in kindergarten, she sent a remark in my direction, "Daddy, some of the other kids' fathers volunteer as classroom helpers." I know her well; I saw where she was going with this.

"Do you want me to sign up as a classroom helper?" I asked.

"Yes," she replied. Carley will make a great salesperson; she's not afraid to ask for the business.

And so I began the process of matching my calendar with the classroom helper coordinator. We finally secured a date in May—a week before school let out. The morning of my class assignment, I had a lot on my mind. Driving down the highway toward my daughter's school, my thoughts were everywhere but in the present. In reality I was fixated on June, which was shaping up to be one of my busiest months, including significant out-of-town travel. I was thinking about phone calls to return, speeches to prepare, paperwork to complete, articles to write, and clients to serve. I was not focused on my role as classroom helper for Carley.

Upon arrival at Carley's school, Ms. Owens (the best kindergarten teacher of all time) greeted me. She asked me to sit in a chair too small for a grown man's gluteus maximus and then help each student read through a phonics workbook. There were sixteen students in Carley's class. Let me be honest: I was not there for the other fifteen children—I only showed up for Carley. Now, I admire people who love all children globally. I am not one of them. In this world I love only two children, and they're both mine. I will not harm other children; I just do not love them. The thought of reading the same phonics book over and over, sixteen times, frightened me. I was wishing Ms. Owens would change her mind and perhaps ask me to clean toilets in the bathrooms. I would have been happier with that assignment, but no such luck.

One by one, the children found their way to the phonics reading area. Then something changed. Actually, I began to change. I started to become enthusiastic about the success the students were having. The boys and I started exchanging high-fives, energy began to grow, and we started having fun. When it was all over, there was genuine excitement from the phonics reading section. If awards were given to classroom helpers, I very well might have received MVH (most valuable helper).

Sitting here today, I can't remember much about June of that year. The places I traveled, the business conducted, and the speeches and workshops delivered are all a distant blur. But I'll never forget the time spent with Carley's kindergarten class teaching six-year-olds how to read; it's etched onto my mind and heart. Meaningful things happened the day I decided to accept

Meaningful things happened the day I decided to step into her world. Engagement happened.

my daughter's challenge and step into her world. Engagement happened. Souls, hearts, and minds were changed. I was changed. Let's dig into your third fundamental principle: **Make It Personal.**

Step Into Their World

When I recommend the principle of *Make it Personal* to leaders, I am often greeted with a common response, "That's great, Rich. I fully support this concept. As a matter of fact…" Then they repeat a phrase that has been circulating among leaders for sometime now. "I make myself totally available to my people. I have an *open-door policy.*" Let me ask you, what the heck is an open-door policy? Why do you need a policy like that anyway? That's got to be one of the dumbest phrases I've ever heard.

Can you imagine a parent saying to their young child, "Okay, son. Daddy's here for you. In fact, Daddy has an open-door policy. Any time you need to see or speak to me, feel free to come on in. Otherwise, I'll see you around." You might be thinking, "In my company I'm not leading children. I lead adults." Yes…but there are fundamental principles that transcend age, culture, gender, and ethnicity. This is one of those principles.

People need leaders to physically, intellectually, and emotionally step into their worlds and make it personal. Your people need a leader who understands what it's like in their environment. They need a leader willing to remove his butt from that cushy office chair, lift his head from the pile of reports, turn away from his technology, and walk on out of that open door. Relationships begin with *Let Them In,* as discussed in the previous chapter, and then must be complemented with an equal portion of this next idea: *you're important enough for me to Make It Personal.*

In engaged cultures, leaders don't wait for people to show up in their office; engaging leaders *pursue* others. It's part of your role. You have the authority. You are in charge. It is not their job to go after you; you must be committed to stepping out of your world and engaging them on their terms and on their turf.

A client of mine works for a global manufacturer. One day I overheard a conversation as his team referred to the "executive floor." I could tell by the tone of voice that this was not an endeared place. It's where the high-level corporate executives reside. It is a sacred space, reserved only for those deemed worthy by their title. Edicts and commands flow from this floor, but their actions demonstrate that they are out of touch with the world of their employees. They keep to themselves—under the guise of an open-door policy. They have emotionally and physically separated themselves from those they lead. As a result, the other employees have disengaged from the executive floor "leaders." It's a shame.

Here's what you can do about it. Become a student of your people. Yes, a student. Study them. Pay attention to them. Listen to them. Learn from them. Ask them questions. Listen some more. Become aware of who they are and what they like. Do you know what type of leadership they will flourish under? Do you know how they feel about your current leadership? Do you know what's really important in their lives? Do you know the names of their significant others or their children?

Do you know what they love to do in their spare time? Do you know of an important accomplishment in their life of which they are particularly proud? Do you know of a time in their life that they had to overcome a challenge or struggle? *Find out.* Get out of your office and into their physical, emotional, and spiritual world. By doing this you will begin earning their commitment and loyalty—and that, my friend, is priceless.

The Power of Praise and Appreciation

Sixty-five percent of Americans received no praise or recognition in the workplace last year, a Gallup poll reported. None. Nada. Yet, the U.S. Department of Labor notes that the number-one reason people leave organizations is because they don't feel appreciated. Another Gallup study of nearly five million employees reveals that increased occurrences of recognition and praise in the workplace can lead to lower turnover, higher customer satisfaction scores, and increased overall productivity. Sounds like engagement to me.

By pursuing your people and becoming students of them, you have the opportunity to reverse this trend and offer one of life's most valuable gifts: honest, sincere praise and appreciation. Mary Kay Ashe, founder of Mary Kay Cosmetics, said, "The two things people want more than sex and money are praise and appreciation." This principle helped her create and foster an engaging culture that has led to a highly successful global business.

LISTENING TO THE EXPERTS

How do you get into their world?

"If my department managers never see me out of my office, they will assume that's the way they run their departments: go to your office and close the door. The 'management by walking around' you hear talked about so much is, in fact, the only way to manage. It takes extra time and it takes transparency. In our company, if my managers go two or three days without seeing me on the floor, they come and ask what's wrong! So you build an expectation among your people, and then you have to stay consistent with that."

—Jeff Burkett, President
Advanced Direct Inc.

"What I did was create a bond of loyalty and trust through open, sincere, and honest communication with my team. I try to always see more in my team than they see in themselves and stay focused on action. Our saying is, 'Well done is better than well said.' We get results and seem to like each other as a team. I recall a time when an executive peer told me, 'You are loyal to your team to a fault. You have to learn to separate yourself from the people on the floor.' Even if this hurts you in the short run, you just can't engage a team by separation—it can't happen."

—Frank Middlebury, former Vice President
of Supply Chain, Fortune 500 Company

After acknowledging the power of sincere praise and appreciation, I will often ask my clients why it's in such short order. Why don't we experience it more often? It can't be the cost, because encouragement is virtually free. I've heard a number of responses. "I never received much of it from my leaders, so I am uncomfortable providing it for those who report to me." Or, "I'm afraid if I start praising my people, then they'll expect it all the time." Or, "What if they think I am doing it only to get something from them? They might feel like I'm attempting to manipulate them." These are all valid concerns.

Let's deal with these common challenges head on. The lack of a role model to demonstrate genuine praise feedback can be a challenge. I'll address that shortly by providing you with a simple template to follow. This will be your opportunity to break the cycle of holding back on such a powerful experience. You can be the one to model this skill for those who follow you.

Fearing that people will begin to expect an inordinate amount of praise from you is unfounded. Listen, we have a serious challenge: people are experiencing a shortage of honest and sincere appreciation. Let's not ignore this because of an unrealistic fear. This core human need will not be met on its own. If you do this right, of course people will want more of it. It's your job to observe them and know them well enough to provide honest insight into their strengths and unique abilities on a regular basis.

The third objection is the possibility of manipulation. I was onsite with one of my client teams recently, and we were working on strengthening internal relationships. At that moment we were practicing a questioning/communication template to help them know and understand each other better when a woman spoke up: "This feels like I'm interrogating my partner; isn't this a way to manipulate people?" My answer was, "Yes, it is…if you're a manipulator."

Let's set the record straight: a tool, technique, or skill has no "spirit" or personality of its own. It takes on the spirit and personality of its user. You determine if a process is used for good or evil. You make it sincere or manipulative. If you are sincere and genuine, the offering of praise will be delivered that way. A leader who uses praise and appreciation as a manipulation tool is ultimately discovered and his or her culture is often irreparably damaged. Be conscious of the need for honest and sincere praise and appreciation. Develop the skills to meet that need. Providing this model for those who follow you will be a great gift.

It's Free and It Works

Do you have a special place at work or at home where you stash personal notes that you've received over the years? Do you keep a neatly preserved stack of thank-you notes, congratulations cards, or perhaps special birthday wishes? When you conduct your spring-cleaning, do those cards and notes remain safe and out of harm's way? Have you ever saved a voice mail and listened to it over and over again because the words you heard were encouraging or appreciative? Why is that?

Back when I was in the health and fitness business, we were building a new family wellness center, complete with a nutritionally focused bistro café. Needing a registered dietitian to help get our food service off the ground, we were lucky to find Nikki to fill that role. She agreed to get the restaurant up and running and then switch her focus toward working with our members and their dietary concerns, since this was her primary training and first love.

Nikki worked hard. I watched her hire the food service staff, open the bistro, close it down, make sandwiches, order food, and take the trash out to the dumpster late at night. Often, before departing for the evening, I would leave Nikki a voicemail telling her how much I appreciated her commitment

Often, before departing for the evening, I would leave Nikki a voicemail telling her how much I appreciated her commitment.

and dedication to our organization and particularly the bistro. I mentioned how I had observed her taking out the trash or spending the extra time required to properly train her staff.

Unfortunately, our bistro plans did not pan out, no fault to Nikki. Our venture into food service had a steep learning curve, and breakeven was taking longer than anticipated. In the meantime, Nikki was offered a job within her field— she would be doing what she loved and was trained for. She wisely said yes to her new opportunity.

After working her two-week notice, we had a going-away party for Nikki. The next morning I entered my office and observed my voicemail light blinking. While reviewing the messages, I noticed one was from Nikki. When I heard her voice, I immediately thought, *Uh oh! Here are her parting comments. She left this message on her way out after her final day. This is her chance to vent any frustrations she might have encountered while working with me.*

As I braced myself for the potential criticism, this is what I heard: "Rich, thanks for the party this evening. Before I go, I want to give you some advice. Don't ever stop the encouraging voicemails. They mean the world to all of us who have received them. Please keep them going after I'm gone. Good luck!" Wow. At that very moment the power of genuine praise and recognition was made crystal clear to me. It hadn't cost me a dime—yet it left a lasting mark on the people I led.

Using the T-A-CT Praise Template

Providing effective praise and appreciation means you've got to pay attention to your people. You must be an observer of good. By paying attention and studying your team, you have the framework to "make it personal." You can offer genuine praise in several areas, using the acronym T-A-CT. The first area is *Things*. This is when you recognize someone for his or her new car, new house, new haircut, great outfit, and so on. We all like to hear others affirm that what we've bought or have is good. As long as this is delivered with a sincere and genuine spirit, it is valuable and useful. It makes others feel good while demonstrating that you are paying attention to them.

The second area is *Accomplishments*. Here, you can recognize someone for completing a degree or certification. Perhaps you recognize her for closing a new deal with a tough client, obtaining a promotion, or winning her adult softball league championship. Again, what makes this effective is that you paid attention to something she has accomplished and you're genuinely happy for her.

The third area is *Character Traits*. This is where you can deliver the greatest impact—because you can't be effective here without being a student of your people. At this level you recognize a particular characteristic or trait that you admire in someone. For instance, you might admire her courage, persistence, commitment, kindness, patience, wisdom, maturity, or insight. Once you determine the trait or quality you appreciate, back it up with evidence. In other words, when and where have you seen this quality demonstrated? This piece is critical. It lends credibility to your praise and proves that you're not making this up out of thin air.

The Praise Template
Things.
***A**ccomplishments.*
***C**haracter **T**raits.*

Finally, be brief and to the point. Allow a moment for the person to say thank you and then move on. Here is the template:

1. Tell the individual what quality or character trait you admire in her.
2. Cite the evidence or specific situation where you observed this trait.
3. Finish by saying, "I wanted to let you know that I admire this about you."
4. Allow a moment for her "Thank you."
5. Shut up. This is critical. Don't ruin the moment by talking incessantly for the next five minutes. When you're done—be done.

Here's an example:

Mary, I really admire how you're willing to patiently listen to people. You demonstrated this when dealing with the irate customer yesterday. I noticed how you allowed him to talk through his experience until he began to feel better. He even left happy after interacting with you. I appreciate this trait in you and your commitment to making our team and our organization a better place.

Although you can provide the power of praise and recognition for someone in ten to fifteen seconds and it's virtually free, most employees are never thanked for the job they do where they work—especially not by their manager. You have an opportunity and a responsibility to change this by consistently providing feedback to your employees when they do good work. Predetermine that you will find and recognize something good each day in others.

You can provide sincere personal praise in the hallway, in a group meeting, in a voicemail, in a handwritten thank-you note, by e-mail, or at the end of each day when you leave. Better yet, go out of your way to share and amplify good news right when it occurs—even if it means interrupting someone to thank her for a great job she has done. By taking the time to say you noticed them and appreciate your employee's efforts, those efforts—and the results they engender—will continue.

Creating and fostering an engaging environment is a contact sport. It requires you to walk out of your office door and come in contact with those who look to you for guidance. Put on your imaginary helmet, mouthpiece, and cleats and get out there. They're waiting for you. They're hoping you'll notice and recognize them. Be present and available, make it personal, and watch something meaningful happen.

Recommended Action Steps

❖ Schedule (yes, I wrote *schedule*) time to walk around. Put it in your Daytimer, in your Outlook calendar, or in your iPad—wherever you keep important appointments. Treat this commitment as if it were immovable and impenetrable. Then, stand up and walk around. Observe and recognize the good you see. Ask questions and listen intently. Do this at least one hour per day.

❖ Make a commitment to learn one new thing about those you lead each week. Find out what their middle names are, where they grew up, what pets they have, what hobbies they love, why they chose their line of work. Learn something new for the sake of knowing them better. Have the courage to ask. If they sense you want to know them better, they'll feel honored.

❖ Praise, praise, praise. Write a note, tell them in private, shout it from the hilltop. Let someone know what you've observed, why you admire and appreciate her, then walk away. You'll provide a gift that she'll cherish.

CHAPTER SIX

Take a Stand

A leader who is not passionately devoted to the cause will not draw much commitment from others. The world will make way for someone who knows what he or she wants because there is not much competition when it comes to passionate commitment.

— Laurie Beth Jones

I attended college in the south and was part of a campus ministry program. A local church supported the ministry, which encompassed several area campuses. Two of them were predominantly white while one was predominately black. I really enjoyed the diversity that our fellowship provided; we had a good group of college students who enjoyed building friendships and having fun together.

At the conclusion of each academic year, we had a celebration banquet. This was a time when the guys were busy determining whom they might ask to attend the banquet with them as their date. It was an exciting event for our group. Several weeks before the big occasion in my senior year, we were called into a meeting with our church pastor and another church leader. Apparently, word had gotten out that a few males in our group from the predominately black school were going to ask some of the white females to be their dates for the banquet. This did not sit well with some members from our supporting church. The meeting was designed to encourage us to make the "right" decision and not have the black guys and white girls attend the event as couples.

The presiding leaders lectured our group on how this issue was about being sensitive to those in our church who might feel uncomfortable with black-white mixed dating. They said it was equally important we didn't "damage" our reputation in the community and therefore negatively impact our ability to invite people into our church. In reality, the conversation wasn't about those issues at all; this was about whether we would allow prejudice to infiltrate our campus ministry program.

Deep down inside, something didn't feel right. These were leaders I had respected, leaders with authority and knowledge well beyond me. Still, something in my core beliefs told me this was off target. Nevertheless, I allowed their superior intellect and position of power to override the voice in my soul. As a result, we complied and there were no interracial couples at our end-of-year banquet that spring.

Twenty-five years have passed, and this experience is still vivid in my mind. The leaders of our campus ministry (of which I was one) succumbed to the church leaders in their persuasive speech. From this lesson we uncover your fourth fundamental principle: *Take a Stand.*

I have replayed this incident hundreds of times in my mind. In my internal do-over, the situation plays out like this: I don't allow my youth or naïveté to extinguish the passion of my inner voice—my core values. I call it what

Since that episode, I have committed to honoring the voice within my heart—even when it goes against popular ideas.

it is: prejudice. I am committed to doing the right thing. The other co-leaders are inspired by my courage and take a stand alongside of me. How I wish that were the way it had unfolded, and how I regret not taking a stand on this wrong decision.

Reflecting back, the words of John Eldredge come to my mind from his book *Journey Of Desire*: "Without a deep and burning desire of our own, we will be ruled by the desires of others....The damage, of course, is a life lost unto itself."[20] Since that college episode, I have committed to honoring the voice and desires within my heart—even when they go against the popular ideas.

Engaging leaders are like that: They are clear about who they are. They are willing to take a stand for what's important to them. They're committed to their core beliefs. They are passionate and they take action.

Be Committed

When Taylor was about six, we participated in a program in which families collected money to send to third-world countries for hunger relief. I thought this would be a great opportunity to teach my daughter about the art of giving. At that time, she had a bank with three "silos"—one for spending, one for saving, and one for giving. When she received money, she would split it three ways within her bank.

The program included a brochure from Manna International, the host organization. On the outside of the brochure was a picture of a young, malnourished boy, drinking dirty water from a spigot with a rusty metal cup. Inside was a calendar. Each day had a question followed by instructions. Example:

> May 1: If you have more than one pair of shoes, give five cents.
>
> May 2: If you eat more than one meal per day, give twenty-five cents.

And so on… You get the idea.

Initially, I would announce each morning, "Taylor, get your bank; it's time to do your giving calendar." She would reluctantly obey, hoping that the financial dent to her bank would not be too harsh. It was obvious to me that she was barely compliant with my intent to teach her to be a gracious giver.

About one week into our project, after persuading her to part with a dime from her "giving silo," she stared curiously at the brochure and then asked me a question. "Dad, when we collect all this money, will it help the boy in the picture to buy a shiny new cup?"

I thought, and then responded, "Yes, I bet this money could help him buy a new cup." Taylor pondered a moment and then walked away with a little more pep in her step.

The very next day, she was waiting for me; bank in hand, to read our assignment. "May 9: If you have your own mode of transportation, give twenty-five cents." Quickly, out came a quarter from her bank into our collection pile. *Wow*, I thought. *This is what I call commitment! "May 31: If you live in a house with just one family, give fifteen cents."* Taylor reached into her bank and extracted her fifteen cents. "Dad," she said, "I want to give all of the money in my bank for the boy's new cup!" *Isn't that nice?* I thought. But that's not what the program calls for.

I replied, "Taylor, that sure is thoughtful of you, but the brochure only asks for fifteen cents today. You have done a good job; we are ready to turn your money in. Go ahead and take your bank back to your room." As the teacher and leader, it seemed to me that this lesson was complete.

A few days later, I was in a meeting. The discussion turned to the challenge of leading teams toward meaningful goals and the temptation for people to hold back and not give their all. I was immediately reminded of my last "teaching session" with Taylor. It hit me like a ton of bricks. I hurried back home from my appointment and called for her to come meet me in the living room. I stooped down to her eye level and said, "Taylor, I was wrong; you were right. You should have given it all. I am sorry I stopped you. Whenever you believe so strongly in something again, go ahead and give everything you've got." She had become the teacher and I the student.

What a lesson on commitment I had just learned. Taking a stand for a deep belief may cost you. It may cost more than you initially bargained for. With Taylor, it began as a belief that she could make a difference for a boy in a far-off land. That belief overcame her initial feeling of compliance, blooming into committed action—*Give it all*. Mary Crowley said, "One person with a commitment is worth a hundred who only have an interest."[21]

Model Commitment

I was meeting with a prospective client a few years ago. It was a 911 call: he needed to meet right away to discuss his staff's lack of commitment and performance. After an hour of listening to his blistering account of their ineptness, I was ready to suggest some initial steps we could take. Before I could do that, he said (with all seriousness), "I'm not going to have to hug my people or anything like that, am I?" I forget how I actually responded in that moment, but I know how I will respond to similar questions in the future. I will lean real close to the prospect, look him or her in the eyes, and firmly ask, "If that's what it takes, are you in?"

This guy wasn't committed to being the engaging leader his people needed; he was more interested in remaining in his comfort zone. He wouldn't take a stand for his team if it meant taking a risk. Therefore, his people would never commit to him. Committed leaders focus on what they are willing to do for their people, not what they're unwilling to do. You can begin to foster an engaging culture by knowing what's important to your followers and then taking a stand on their behalf.

❋ ❋ ❋

"If that's what it takes, are you in?"

❋ ❋ ❋

One of the strongest leaders I've had the privilege of working beside is Sally Newton. Not long after transplanting from Pennsylvania to North Carolina, she built a booming, profitable, and meaningful business, both for her customers and her staff.

After a merger of our two organizations, Sally became one of my partners, and I admired her blend of northern toughness and southern tenderness. There came a time when she needed to have a one-on-one meeting with a staff member, Jerry, who was struggling with telling the truth. She asked me to sit in on the meeting as a witness to the conversation. Sally began by pointing out some of the strengths she saw in Jerry. Then, without any warning, she said, "Jerry, let's talk about some of the lies you've been telling." I immediately slouched in my chair, took note of the intricate carpet patterns, and thought, *Holy cow. She just called him a liar!*

They continued the conversation to better understand Jerry's behavior and what might be driving it. He never denied it or tried to get around the allegations. Despite the challenging topic, they came away with a plan that would make things better, and on his way out, Jerry turned and thanked her for her feedback.

Here's what I learned from Sally that day: if people are convinced you have their best interest in mind, they will listen to you, even when it's tough. When Sally hired someone, she demonstrated a commitment to the person immediately. She believed in him and took a stand for him. He could see and feel it. She became a trusted advisor to her staff. The way Sally saw it, her top priority was to create an engaging atmosphere of trust and rapport, letting others know that they were important to her. The result was an uncanny loyalty from employees who were, in turn, committed to her and the organization.

How do you reap commitment from others? Sow it first. Just like Sally Newton did.

What would you empty your "bank" for? What would the people in your organization say you take a stand for? What are you committed to or passionate about? Want your people to demonstrate commitment to you and your organization? Dare to show them what that looks like.

LISTENING TO THE EXPERTS

What does commitment look like in your organization?

"I'm the first one in the office and the last to leave. Whatever it takes to get the job done, I do it (e.g., straighten magazines, change toilet paper, etc.). We conduct a morning huddle from 7:45 to 7:55 each morning. It's not a bitch session; rather, we look ahead for upcoming opportunities or potential speed bumps, and then we read something inspirational. We celebrate special events and birthdays. Each of our staff has special uniforms personally monogrammed. We learn and read books together and attend professional development seminars. We recognize the personal challenges that all of our staff are wrestling with, and we don't shy away from them. I never ask my team to leave their personal problems at home. That's a dysfunctional concept. They understand that they can bring their whole self to work. I listen to them and understand. Then we get to work and make magic happen."

—Mark Hyman, DDS

"I had five people in our operations come up to my production manager and say, 'We understand what is going on. We know we need to keep costs down.

We'll work tomorrow off the clock.' Now, they didn't realize that we can't do that; it's against the law. But I think that speaks volumes about their commitment to the success of the company. They make the connection between their success and the company's success, which is huge! We're getting great ideas from our line workers about things we can do to keep costs down— things that we've never heard before. It's because of that level of commitment I just described."

—Jeff Burkett, President
Advanced Direct Inc.

Act Upon Your Dreams

Who will take a stand for you? Who will act on your behalf? Look in the mirror. That's who. People trust you by what they see you do, not merely by what they hear or read about you. W. H. Murray writes this in *The Scottish Himalayan Expedition*:

Concerning all acts of initiative (and creation), there is one elementary truth, the ignorance of which kills countless ideas and splendid plans: that the moment one definitely commits oneself, then providence moves too. All sorts of things occur to help one that would not otherwise have occurred. A whole stream of events issues from the decision, raising in one's favour all manner of unforeseen incidents and meetings and material assistance which no man would have dreamed would come his way. I have learned a deep respect for one of Goethe's couplets:"Whatever you can do, or dream you can, begin it. Boldness has a genius, magic, and power in it. Begin it now."[22]

When you take a stand for your own deep belief, things happen. You are not alone. The entire universe responds and works on your behalf, cheering you on toward success. Let's talk about how you can start by taking a stand for your dreams.

First you must get clear on what your dreams are. Then, write them down. Tell others about them and begin to act upon them. Finally ask someone you trust to support you toward those dreams. Your dreams will inspire some to follow you and others to have the courage to follow their own. Either way, everyone is better off.

At six thirty on a warm July morning I witnessed a dream take off. I watched with mixed emotions as my then sixteen-year-old daughter boarded a flight bound for a six-month student exchange program in Chile. In the weeks to come, I once again found myself in a role reversal with one of my daughters. Taylor had become the teacher and I the student.

Taylor's dream had begun taking shape years before. During numerous trips to visit family in New Jersey and New York, she fell in love with the variety of language, food, and culture that exists throughout our country. She knew one day she would explore this great and diverse world. Taylor worked tirelessly to conquer the potential barriers to her dream: she researched online, filled out paperwork, traveled to meetings, and gave up lots of personal time to work and save money.

After Taylor left the country, it was almost five anxiety-filled days before I could connect with her. Once she settled in with her host family, I eagerly dialed their phone number in Arica, Chile. After stumbling through the phrase, "*Hola, may I speak with Taylor Schlentz, please*" in my best Spanish-Jersey accent, Taylor was summoned to the phone. I couldn't wait to hear her voice filled with the sounds of excitement and adventure.

"Hello, Dad," was all she could muster before bursting into tears. "This is so hard!" she sniffed. Her dream was tougher than she had imagined. The best I could do was cry along with her and assure her that her emotions were appropriate and to be expected. I encouraged her that soon those feelings would give way to those of wonder and thrill.

And finally they did. In an e-mail dated August 24, Taylor wrote, "I really think this is the perfect experience for me. I just keep thinking when I am walking down the streets here, how lucky I am and how I am so blessed. It's really given me an amazing perspective, and I love it. I love you." Quite different from our phone conversation six weeks earlier.

Here's what I learned from my daughter about acting on our dreams: (1) *Your dreams are meant to fly*. No barrier is insurmountable to the person who has a clear and compelling vision of who she must be or what she must accomplish. It is only a matter of getting on the runway and putting the throttle down. If dreams don't take off,

What I learned...
Your dreams are meant to fly.
Your dreams will test you.
Your dreams will bless you.

they die on the tarmac of lost intentions. Your strong belief can be the thrust your dreams need to take flight.

(2) *Your dreams will test you.* Dan Allender writes, "Dreams can quickly become fantasies if we refuse to risk and bleed for our future."[23] Expect to pay a price for your dreams. Buckle up and anticipate turbulence. It's part of the flight pattern. Your journey, along with your destination, will change you forever.

(3) *Your dreams will bless you.* If you stay with it, your dreams will provide some amazing perspectives. If you let them fly, while expecting the occasional challenges and fears, you will eventually marvel at the depth and meaning they add to your life journey.

I have often said, "The only differences between men and boys are that men grow taller and have lost their dreams." Now I realize I was wrong. You can't *lose* your dreams, but you can give them away. You can trade them in for someone else's dreams. You can refuse to act on them.

The good news is that you can also reclaim them by taking a stand. Just grab your "dream e-ticket," head to the dream counter, and proclaim, "I want my dream seat—preferably next to the window." Then buckle up. I'll see you in the clouds.

Your Oxygen First

Speaking of flight, if you have ever flown in an airplane, you've experienced the boring safety announcement. Although you may have only paid attention during your first flight, can you recall what to do if the cabin pressure drops and the oxygen masks fall from the overhead compartment? What are you supposed to do with that oxygen mask? You put the mask over your face first and then help the person beside you. That seems selfish, doesn't it? No, we all get it. If you don't have oxygen for yourself, you're not going to be much help to others. Why does that make so much sense at thirty thousand feet, yet it's a struggle once you return to sea level? Here's the lesson for engaging leaders: Take a stand for your own personal growth and development plan first.

I hear from leaders that they find it difficult to take time out for their own development and well-being. The result is "oxygen-deprived" leaders who have very little left over to give to others. *A Course In Miracles* wisely states, "Who can bestow upon another what he does not have? And who can share what he denies himself?"[24]

I'm in the professional development industry. I help people create a vision to grow into their highest self. I hold them accountable to follow through. I constantly remind them how important this is, not only for themselves but also for those who follow. I help them overcome the constant barrage of obstacles that seemingly rise up to prevent them from moving forward.

That being said, I find that at times I neglect my own development. I can allow myself to be distracted by the "good work" I do for others. I can rationalize that I'm growing my business and will take a rain check for myself. Resist this trap.

I'm talking about an engaging leader striking the delicate balance of self and others. Be committed to both yourself and others. One is not more important than the other. Both are of tremendous value. You need oxygen and so do they. If in a particular moment you must make a choice, remember, you can't share what you deny yourself. You're worth it. You need it. Those who follow you will benefit from this example in you.

In his book, *Man's Search For Meaning*, Victor Frankl writes, "For success, like happiness, cannot be pursued; it must ensue, and it only does so as the unintended side-effect of one's personal dedication to a cause greater that oneself."[25]

So it is with living the life of an engaging leader. It cannot be pursued; it must ensue. It manifests from your dedication to take a stand for your inner voice, your dreams, and your personal development. Becoming an engaging leader is also the result of demonstrating your commitment to those you lead. Being recognized as an engaging leader is an outgrowth of your bias toward action. This takes courage. This takes dedication. When you do these, you'll be a rare leader—a leader who understands not only himself but also his people…and that's where we're headed in our next chapter.

Recommended Action Steps

❖ What are you willing to take a stand for? What deep belief and passionate cause do you represent? Get clear on that by writing it down. Don't meander through life half-committed. I can say without a doubt that I am called to the souls, hearts, and minds within our global workplace. It's my ministry. How about you? What and whom are you willing to fight for?

❖ How do you show your commitment to those you lead? Do they feel that you're committed to them? How about asking them? Have a one-on-one conversation with a few of your key followers. Ask, "In what ways do I demonstrate my commitment to you? How could I improve?" Listen and learn.

❖ Grab hold of your oxygen mask and take a hit. Make a list of the things you'll do for you. What steps can you take to fulfill your dreams? What learning experience will help you grow and develop as an engaging leader? Invest in yourself. Then you'll have the reserves needed to serve and build others.

CHAPTER SEVEN
Seek and Ye Shall Understand

A person who seems to have all the answers usually isn't listening.

– Jeffrey Gitomer

I was at an upscale county club working with thirty people from a successful auto dealership. The audience included managers and department heads from across the organization. We were discussing and practicing the skill of impactful listening. The general manager from the company's most successful dealership blurted out, "Rich, I've got to be honest. When I'm listening to an employee or a customer, I often find myself thinking that I've heard all of this before. It's the same old story over and over again, and it drives me nuts."

I let his comment sink in for a moment before I replied. "Joe, at times it can be tiresome to listen intently to others, especially when we have a lot on our plate. Let's consider another way to look at this. Sometimes the stories people are sharing with us can sound similar. Yet perhaps they're all unique, much like the people speaking them. Could it be that we tend to be listening with the same old set of tired ears?"

As a general manager, Joe struggled with intently listening to his people, and this was a detriment to his leadership. People resisted following him, and as a result, Joe didn't last much longer at this company. He was an expert in his industry with years of experience. Yet knowledge alone doesn't engage people; it's our ability to connect with them as human beings. Part of that is a willingness to understand others—and that requires the discipline of asking and listening.

The point is simple. Understand those you lead and serve; they need you to understand them. It's your job to study your people and know them well. It's your job to supply the right questions, to listen intently, and gain the understanding needed to lead effectively. You might be able to manage people you don't really know, but you can't lead someone you don't understand. That's why your fifth fundamental principle is *Seek and Ye Shall Understand.*

By genuinely seeking to understand a person, you pay him or her one of life's highest compliments. This is not only about seeking to know *something*; it's also about seeking to know *someone*. It is possible to know about someone and not know *him*. Think about it. Sometimes knowledge is not enough. True understanding goes deeper than knowledge: it's embedded in sincerity and focused on the desire to see things from the other person's point of view. The best way to do that is by creating an environment that is conducive to understanding.

Understanding someone is not passive. It doesn't happen *to* you; you go after it. The Bible says, "Ask and it will be given to you; seek and you will find; knock and the door will be opened to you" (Matt. 7:7). To really understand someone takes action—like asking, seeking, and knock-

❖ ❖ ❖

It is in the active pursuit of a relationship that we acquire understanding.

❖ ❖ ❖

ing. It is in the active pursuit of a relationship that we acquire genuine understanding.

While you seek to understand someone, it helps if you'll eliminate the need to be right. That's a burden worth dumping. If your objective is to be right by proving someone else wrong, don't be surprised when you simultaneously find yourself alone. Even in sharing your opinions, you can let go of the desire to change someone or make her see things your way. Rumi, the eleventh-century poet and scholar, penned, "Out beyond the ideas of wrongdoing and rightdoing, there is a field. I'll meet you there."[26] How refreshing. You can build a culture in which mutual understanding is more important than right and wrong. Your team will eagerly meet you there.

Stop Knowing—Start Asking

I suppose it was because I thought I was so smart. Perhaps I believed that asking was a sign of weakness. Instead of asking questions, I would constantly grasp for the right answer. Maybe I didn't trust people to give me the right answer—even when it concerned them. Whatever the reason, for the majority of my life, I pretended to know most of the answers. This trait did not serve me well.

I finally decided to let go of the answers and replace them with questions. I have released myself from the need to appear all-knowing, and let me tell you, I'm a lot happier. The burden is lighter. I feel free. Free from needing to have the answers to everything and for everyone. Free from having it all figured out. The Bible says that the truth will set you free.[27] To tell you the truth, letting go of all my "answers" has set me free.

Now, when I don't know something, I ask. Then...I listen. Ultimately, I understand. I've stopped guessing and started exploring, and as a result, I am a more effective leader, friend, dad, and husband. You can experience this, too.

"Knowing" can be a trap and a curse. Oh yeah, it feels good to know—at least for a while, until it has you bound so tight that you can't see how you'll ever escape its grasp. As kids, we never liked the neighborhood know-it-all. Somehow, along the way, a lot of us have morphed into that villain. Let's take a look at the common "knowing" model for leadership:

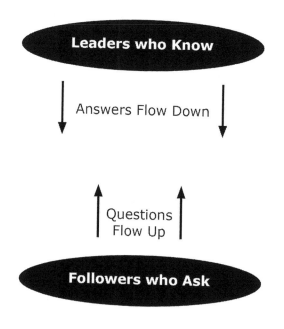

This is one of the most common communication models I observe leaders utilizing, and it's simple to understand why. It's what got you here. It's the process that made you an expert in your field. It's what others admired about you. "If you ever need a quick answer, just ask Bill."

This model is highly ineffective for leaders. It has a limited shelf life. It begets exhaustion and codependency; it's ultimately an unhealthy model. You need followers to ask questions (which makes you feel important and smart), and they need you to give them the answers (which justifies their false belief that they are not smart enough and that their ideas are unimportant).

Leaders end up bitter because they never get a break. Even at home, they are interrupted because someone somewhere needs an answer. If you are that leader, you probably get angry, wondering why your employees can't figure out the answers to their own problems. The real problem is you haven't given them ownership of those problems. You insist on owning them yourself. Your followers become resentful because they don't see themselves as vital to the organization's success. They don't feel that their contribution is valued. Ultimately, they cease contributing, become disengaged, and quit—they just don't leave.

Let's consider a new "asking" model for leadership interaction:

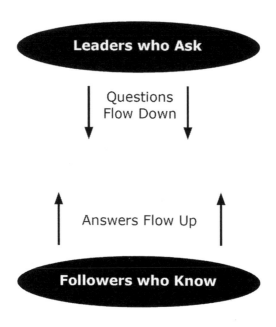

See the difference? Ahhh, what a relief. You're finally off the answer hook. This model allows you to fulfill one of your most important roles—building up others by becoming a masterful questioner. In *The Question Behind The Question,* author John G. Miller writes, "Leaders are not problem solvers but problem givers. They let others tackle the problem, design their own solutions, and take action. How else can people learn?"[28]

Allow others the opportunity to provide their answers. Cease enabling this dysfunction. Break the unhealthy code-pendent model we discussed earlier. When you focus on leading, building, and creating an engaging culture, your followers are free to bring their knowledge and talents to the workplace and make a difference for the organization. This is good. Break the pattern of knowing and telling. Replace it with asking and listening. You'll reap understanding, and your followers will gladly provide better ideas than you can think of alone.

One of the premises necessary to execute this is the belief that your followers do indeed have answers. In fact, you must be convinced that they are as smart as you—perhaps even smarter in specific areas. This personal belief takes root in the soil of self-confidence. In other words, it takes confidence to release your knowingness and ask questions.

The Answer Is in the Question

As with everything in this book, you can't wait on someone else; change begins with you. If this belief doesn't burn deep within you, then change will be too tough for you. The pain of remaining the same must be greater than the pain of change. The ability to gain understanding through skillful questioning is supported by a sincere curiosity to know others in a deeper way, the desire to help them uncover the answers they already possess. If that is the case for you, then you will do the necessary work involved...but it may be one of your toughest assignments.

In his book, *Velvet Elvis*, Rob Bell writes, "Questions are not scary. What is scary is when people don't have them. Questions bring freedom."[29] I've had the opportunity to mentor under a world-class questioner: Emily Howard has been my friend and business colleague. She is also a great salesperson...not because she greets potential clients with facts, benefits, and information about what she does and who she is. Emily's plan is always the same. *What questions will I ask? What do I need to learn? How can I better understand this buyer and their needs?* She skillfully questions and listens her way to the sale. For Emily, strategic questioning and listening means revenue. It works for her. It can work for you.

We're *all* in sales. Leaders have to be top-notch sales-people to sell their visions, beliefs, ideas, concepts, plans, and products. Success in this area isn't necessarily about asking more questions; it's about asking *better* questions.

Gaining Understanding

Here's a tool called Grasp The Situation (GTS), including sample questions that I use with clients or staff. The intent is always the same: to arrive at better understanding of any person or situation.

Grasp the Situation (GTS)

Current State
Tell me about your situation.
How did this come about?
What is your role in this?
How have you contributed?

Future Ideal
How should things be different?
What would be ideal?
What should your role be?

Meaning
What is this issue or this ideal important to you?
What would this mean to you personally?

Prevent
What might prevent you from achieving your ideal? What else?

Require
What's it going to take to accomplish this?

I begin meetings with a blank sheet of paper and start asking GTS questions. I then listen and ask more questions for greater clarity. When the conversation is complete, the blank paper is typically full with the person's thoughts, answers, and truths. The questions are aligned into four quadrants. Your starting point is *Current State*. Understanding what has happened up unto this point is critical. It is important in any conversation that you understand the "road to now." Have the person you're speaking with paint a picture of what things currently look like. And don't move ahead until you see it as clearly as he or she does.

Next, shift to the *Future Ideal*. Find out what the person wants to be different or how she would like to encounter the future. This is her vision—let her articulate a "picture" of her ideal world or experience.

Now you've created a gap. There is a chasm between where she is and where she'd like to be—the current and the future. One of your callings as a leader is to help others build a bridge between their current reality and their desired future.

Although you can't travel for her, you can assist this person in creating her own journey to an ideal outcome. Begin asking the third quadrant questions: What might *prevent* her from arriving at this outcome? What might block her from achieving her ideal state?

Subsequently, have her think and articulate *what will be required of her to create her future ideal? What will it take?* This will necessitate that she take responsibility for her actions and outcomes. Knowing what the journey will require of her will clarify the support needed. You are not responsible for her success or failure. You are responsible for providing the necessary resources and tools that will help her succeed.

The final quadrant, *Meaning,* deals with the heart. Movement and action begin in the heart. People "do" because of emotion. In sales, we say that people buy emotionally and justify logically. The question *What would this mean to you personally?* takes courage to ask. Often, the first response you receive will sound "corporate" and be a surface answer. Because you are courageous and an engaging leader, you will ask again, "And what will that mean to you *personally*?" Don't retreat. Stick with them. Understanding why this is important at their heart level is critical. When they allow you into this place, you are earning their trust.

Working the Process

Here's how this looks in action. A few years ago I began working with a local community bank. My client was Bonnie Jones, vice president. Bonnie contacted me because she was interested in a training program for her midlevel managers. Now, I've been selling for a long time and I know that nobody wants to buy training. People really want what the training or new skill might provide them. It's my job to understand what potential clients are actually interested in buying. The best way to get clear on that is to use the GTS template and gain understanding.

My first goal was to understand her *current state*, which consisted of leading about fifteen midlevel managers. One of the strengths her bank possessed was the ability to attract and keep good people, and as a result it had a strong collection of up-and-coming leaders. As a group, they currently lacked a mastery of fundamental leadership skills, and Bonnie wanted this to change.

I then asked what her managers would be doing differently or better when they obtained and applied some of these effective leadership tools. What would her *future ideal* midlevel manager "look like"? She stated that they would have greater confidence in their abilities. Not only would they have more of an impact on the bank's financial success by being great at what they do, they would also be building the people around them. She could imagine them communicating clearly and effectively, listening to their direct reports, providing tools others needed for success…on and on she went. Her ideal state for guiding and building her managers was clear and compelling.

When Bonnie was asked what might *prevent* them from accomplishing the future ideal for her managers, she replied, "Nothing. I will make sure this happens. It's too important to neglect or allow to get sidetracked." Great answer. Bonnie takes a stand for her followers—she earns loyalty as a result of this.

"Well, Bonnie, *what's it going to take* to make this happen?" I asked.

"Commitment and follow through," she replied. "I'm committed and will make sure we follow through on informing the managers about the benefits of our program and scheduling the necessary learning modules." One of the characteristics I admire about Bonnie is that she takes personal responsibility for making things happen.

Lastly, I leaned forward in my chair, lowered my voice, looked directly into Bonnie's eyes, and asked, "Bonnie, when we accomplish your vision for the managers, *what will that mean to you*?" As if on automatic pilot, she began spewing corporate verbiage. Long-term growth, shareholder value, return on investment, and so on. I allowed her to finish and then leaned a little closer. "Bonnie, why is this *important to you personally*?" That's where I hit pay dirt, and that's where the personal meaning question will set you apart from ordinary communicators.

Bonnie began to let me in on a story. Her story. She recalled early on in her banking career how she seemed to be stalled at the mid-manager level. She had aspirations of growing and advancing within her bank and industry. That's when a leader she admired stepped in. He encouraged her to stretch and develop her rough skills. He suggested that she find ways to learn more and improve her abilities. He saw the potential inside of her and didn't want to see it go to waste. This leader left a mark on Bonnie. She is where she is today because of his impact on her years ago.

As I sat and listened, it became crystal clear to me that this project was not about management skills or a world-class learning program. For Bonnie, this was about giving back— leaving her own legacy among a group of people that she was convinced

❖ ❖ ❖

When you accomplish your vision, what will that mean to you?

❖ ❖ ❖

had talent. From that moment on, I had insight into Bonnie and what was important to her. This is a trusted and important place to be. Our entire relationship shifted from training her managers to helping her to leave a legacy.

Dig Deeper

Once you ask skilled questions, you will often find opportunities to follow up and "dig down." Often a single question won't give you the understanding you need. Consider following up by using broad questions with few words. Keep them open-ended, without "steering" the conversation anywhere. Steering is manipulation—that's not for you. Your questions are for gaining insight and understanding. Let others decide where the conversation should go. Let go of conversation control. Pack some "wonder" in your briefcase and ask yourself, "I wonder what makes them feel that way?" Then ask them that very question.

Give yourself permission to be child-like (not childish; there is a big difference) by being curious. Become genuinely inquisitive and interested in other people. The understanding you gain will enrich your life and the lives of those around you. Here are some follow-up questions that work well:

- Tell me more about…
- What are the beliefs behind those words or feelings?
- Why do you think that is?
- In what way?
- Give me an example…Help me see what that looks like.
- That word can have a number of different meanings. What does it mean to you?
- How so?
- Help me understand…
- What else?

Recently I had a conversation with a prospective client. She has been in business for years and is beginning a new venture. During our conversation, we uncovered a pattern in which she would take her businesses to a certain level of success and then "hit a wall." Our work together will be about helping her experience a different outcome this time around. Here are some actual questions I e-mailed her. I gave her some time to reflect before we reconvened to move ahead:

> I've been thinking about our conversation and your new journey toward success. Based on the pattern we discovered—building your business to a certain point and then "hitting a wall"—can you give some thought to a few questions?
>
> - What do you see as the root cause of this dynamic?
> - What role have you played in this repeated experience?
> - How have you contributed to the pattern?
> - What makes this the time for you to have a new experience?
> - What will you do differently this time?
> - Why do you deserve success?

As an effective leader building an engaging culture of your own, you can wrestle with similar questions concerning your own desired outcome. Self-questioning is an important part of leadership growth. My favorite is: *What is my role in this?* Depending on your learning style, you may want to ask questions like these to yourself and then sit in silence, allowing the answer to appear in the quiet. Or you may want to sit with a trusted friend and verbally process your personal questions and answers. Another option that might prove useful is to journal your own questions and answers.

One thing is certain: Asking yourself questions—*What is my role in this? What do I like about how things turned out? What would I have liked to be different? What will I do differ-*

ently in a similar situation next time?—is an important part of your own self-mastery. The answers you need to hear are already present; it's the questions that are missing. The ability to debrief a situation or incident with good self-discovery questions is a very high level of leadership.

Conversational Fundamentals

Let's finish with some fundamentals. It's time to apply simple, timeless, and effective ways to engage in meaningful conversations that bring you insight and understanding from others. Here are some basics that get results.

Offload prejudice. When asking and listening to others or yourself, it is imperative to be free of judgment. We often show up to conversations having prejudged a person or situation. This is simply prejudice. (Yes, they're the same.) Resist this temptation. Before entering into meaningful conversation with skillful questions, take a moment and check your motives. Make sure that your intent is to ask, *listen*, and understand. Clear your mind and heart of any "knowing" or "judgment" that you're already carrying with you.

Shut down technology. Things get in the way of people. Have you noticed that? At times it seems as if we're a society that worships technology and tolerates people. Perhaps the solution is to shut down your technology. I mean it—shut it down. Demonstrate the importance of

Turn off your cell phone. Believe me, you're not that important!

others by not allowing e-mail "alerts" to occur while you're focusing on them and the conversation at hand. Also, turn away from your computer screen. That's right—turn your back on the god of technology; you will feel liberated by this step alone.

LISTENING TO THE EXPERTS

How do you empower your team as a leader?

"You have to be others-oriented. You've got to be caring, available, enthusiastic; you've got to give vision. We really foster teams, so there's an element of locking arms involved. As a leader, I think you have to have the ability to let go and trust your people. For most men who want to be in control and in charge, that's counterintuitive. And I'm perfectly fine with that. You realize that people are going to make mistakes, and that's okay. There's a healthiness of servant leadership about it.

"I think you've got to live it out, you've got to recognize people, you've got to celebrate people. You've got to fertilize the values that we've decided really matter, and so if respect is one of our values and we're not being respectful in how we partner with people here, maybe it's because of my disorganization. Or me being in a hurry and having too much going on. When that happens, I've put people in a bad spot, and that's really not respectful. So I think leaders have got to self-examine and be humble. You've got to think about it and work at it, so there's an element of humility and accountability."

—Brett Grieves, Vice President
Scott Risk & Insurance Services

Now turn off your cell phone (unless your wife is expected to go into labor any minute). There is no reason you can't turn it off; believe me, you're *not* that important. Turning it to vibrate won't cut it; turn it all the way off. By allowing people to observe you do this, you will automatically make them feel more important before you even say a word.

Listen first. When in meetings with your staff, do not begin with your ideas or input. Begin with questions designed to elicit their ideas. If you speak first, you taint their answers. If your meeting questions sound like, "So that's what I think about the situation. What do you guys think we should do?"—understand that you are not hearing their truths but merely a version of I-better-say-something-that-agrees-with-my-boss rubbish. Ask first; resist the temptation to add to or direct the discussion until all of their ideas and potential solutions are out on the table.

Physically engage. Finally, if you're in an office or out to lunch or coffee, face the person. Focus on them with your eyes and energy. Then ask good questions and listen. The results will astound you. You will not regret it.

It is imperative that you have the courage to engage your people with thoughtful, skillful questions, genuine listening, and the gift of understanding. One of our core human needs is to be heard. Your people have something to say. Give them this gift, and reap loyalty and commitment that will last a lifetime.

A while back I saw the movie *August Rush*. It's a movie about listening—primarily listening to the music that surrounds us. It's also about listening to our hearts, our thoughts, and our dreams. The main character is an eleven-year-old boy. In the movie's closing line, he states, "The music is all around us. All you have to do is listen." To that I add: the *answers* are all around you—all you have to do is ask.

Recommended Action Steps

❖ Check your ears. It's not always about what others are saying; it could be about how you're listening. Think about a situation you'll be facing this week. Jot some thoughts down to these questions: *What bias do I bring to the conversation? How might I be prejudging the situation?* Prepare to listen without any desired outcome except to understand.

❖ Lighten your load by letting go of the answers. They may have gotten you here, but they won't take you where an engaging leader needs to go. At your next staff meeting, plan to ask questions first. Listen and take notes. If you must add your input, wait until the end. See yourself as a guide or facilitator with those who follow, not the all-knowing Oz.

❖ Work on your questioning skills. Use the ones recommended in this chapter. Build some of your own. This is tougher than it looks. Do you know someone who is a skilled questioner and listener? Spend time with him and observe. Be curious. Ask to understand. Dig down. Once you begin getting the hang of it, you'll never go back to knowing everything.

CHAPTER EIGHT

Watch Your Mouth

A fool finds no pleasure in understanding but delights in airing his own opinions.

– Proverbs 18:2

When Taylor was in the seventh grade, she brought home one of her end-of-quarter report cards. Let me preface this with a quick fact: at this time both of my daughters had already received more As in their academic careers than I did all the way through graduate school.

Taylor left her report card on the kitchen counter for my review, and I studied it carefully. I noticed that her GPA was 3.78 out of 4.0. Not bad, I thought. Several of her grades had risen since last quarter…nice. Then I spotted it. In two of her eight classes, her behavior score had dropped from an O (outstanding) to an S (satisfactory). *What was going on here? What was she thinking? How could she do this to me?* In my personal score book, this was a U (unsatisfactory). I would have to handle this most unsightly report card swiftly and directly.

The first thing I did was to get my trusty highlighter (this is a true story). I quickly highlighted the behavior grades that had dropped. I wanted to be sure we both could see these hideous results. Then I marched with heavy, deliberate steps to her room and called out, "Taylor, I want to speak with you."

"What went on to change these behavior grades from O to S?" I demanded. She defended her position by saying that overall she was pleased with her report card. But I was bound and determined to confront her with my disappointment, recommending that she come up with an action plan to change these results back to an O next quarter. I walked out of her room leaving her dazed, confused, and deflated. As a dad and leader, I was convinced my point was clearly communicated.

Ten minutes passed before I was struck with an out-of-body experience. I thought to myself, *What on earth have I just done? This kid is smart, respectful, courteous, conscientious, responsible, and a much better student than I have ever been. Why did I feel compelled to seek out the only part of her report card that had not improved and dwell on that? What about me required that type of conversation?*

And that's just it. This issue was about me, not her. I walked back into Taylor's room with my head lowered and asked her to sit on the bed with me, and I began to apologize for my words and actions. My outburst with her reminded me of the Ralph Waldo Emerson quote, "What you are shouts so loudly in my ears I cannot hear what you say."[30] So here's your sixth fundamental principle: **Watch Your Mouth**.

I cringe to think of the long-term effect of those words if I had not retracted them. No doubt, my words stung her. I had shot from the hip, leaving wounds across her heart. Verbal bullets leave their mark. If it weren't for apologies and forgiveness, those wounds might still be aching today.

Shootin' from the Hip Leaves People Wounded

I used to admire those people. You know, the ones who appear so confident and bold when they speak. They say things like, "Hey, I just tell it like it is. I speak my mind. Me, I shoot from the hip! People always know where I stand." I yearned for the courage to speak with such strength and conviction…strutting down the hall like John Wayne, just shootin' from the hip.

I don't feel that way anymore. I know better now. This aggressive, faultfinding communication style is the exact opposite of confidence. As a matter of fact, it stems from a lack of self-confidence, which manifests itself in an aggressive manner.

I've seen managers who hold their direct reports hostage with harsh, cutting words. Managers who use their preference for aggression to scare the creativity and ingenuity out of people who used to be highly productive. The practice of "telling it like it is" or "shooting from the hip" can cause damage and leave bodies in its wake. If you are wounding people with your words, I suggest you stop before you become the target of a mutiny. If people hide in their offices, under their desks, or in the bathroom when you are near, it could be sign that you are a terrorist with your words.

Faultfinding stems from a lack of self-confidence, which manifests itself in an aggressive manner.

Dan Allender encapsulates these thoughts nicely:

Arrogance often masquerades as strength. Many leaders use bluster, bravado, and the fire and magic of the Wizard of Oz to hide their balding, paunchy frailty. Many leaders are highly verbal, and they intimidate their community with the threat of contempt. Team members and employees know well the power of a leader to publicly shame them. This awareness is enough to silence most people since the thought of responding publicly to the taunt terrifies them.[31]

> ## LISTENING TO THE EXPERTS
>
> ### *What is the impact of disengaged employees?*
>
> "There is a significant cost to disengagement. You see turnover in an organization, which is very expensive. You also see lower morale on the team. Low morale equals low productivity. People will work enough to keep their job...but just barely. We need employees who are engaged, knowing that what they do is important and makes a difference!"
>
> —Mary Cloninger, CMPE, Executive Director
> Carolina Neurosurgery & Spine Associates

Put the Gun Down

Here's a lesson I've learned about words—less is more. Listening is more effective than speaking. What I don't say is much more important than what I do say. It is physically and mentally more challenging to hold words back than it is to let them fly. Ultimately, limiting or editing my words takes more skill and maturity than saying the first things that come to mind.

I was sharing this revelation with a friend the other day when it occurred to me that this philosophy might be useful in all areas of my life. If I say less...I might be saying more. Think about it.

Saint Francis of Assisi is attributed with this line: "Preach the Gospel every day. Use words only when necessary."[32] What if, before speaking, you asked yourself, *What do I really need to say here? What do I really want to accomplish? How can I get the results I'm after and still keep the relationship intact?* And the most important question of all: *Is what I am getting ready to say my issue or the other person's?* After you have resolved these questions, consider using words.

Use your words to encourage others. This means that people leave interactions with you having greater courage. They feel more powerful and confident. If your words deflate people, change that. How can you tell? Do people come to you for advice or ask to speak with you about a professional or personal issue? Can you recall the last time someone asked you to sit down and chat because he needed a trusted friend to just listen? If no one ever enters your "open door," chances are that your words may be discouraging instead of encouraging.

Understand, I'm not advocating an "everything must be positive" position on communication. As a leader, it's critical that you demonstrate the ability to see and speak things as they are. If you are going to be a believable leader for others and yourself, reject the temptation to place a positive spin on everything

Corporate America is known for its ability to spin information, and that has damaged the reputation and credibility of many leaders. Words have little meaning when the speaker is viewed as incongruent, inauthentic, or out of touch with reality. Refusing to acknowledge how things really are causes your followers to doubt you.

Can you recall the last time someone asked you to sit down and chat because he needed a trusted friend to just listen?

Stressful circumstances cause people

to be insecure and therefore say stupid things. There are times when clichés don't work and scripted thoughts fail: mergers and acquisitions, challenging economic times, and corporate downsizing fall into this category.

Speaking Things as They Are

Doug was forty-three when he died suddenly of a heart attack. He was a friend I had grown up with and played college soccer with. You couldn't meet or know Doug without being impacted positively. Doug was inclusive, caring, and always looking for the good in others. He was also one heck of a competitor on the soccer field. As general manager of the Los Angeles Galaxy professional soccer team, he had risen to one of the highest levels within the sport he loved. Doug left behind a wife and a five-year-old son when he died. His body was flown from California to North Carolina for the burial. We had a local service, attended by hundreds of the people Doug had touched throughout his life.

When I finally had the chance to speak with his wife, Paige, I held her and said, "I'm sorry. This just sucks." She replied, "You know, I've wanted to say that for several days now. This really does suck." That was a real exchange. Those were real feelings and real words, spoken from our hearts. Not some scripted hand-me-down crap. It felt good to speak the truth, and I think Paige appreciated it also.

The ability to see and communicate things as they are can be difficult. It shouldn't be, but it can be. You're not in control of the universe. You're not responsible for every circumstance that occurs. I received good advice from a friend when he said, "Rich, why don't you resign as general manager of the universe?" That was a powerful recommendation. Your job is to be real, not in control. Part of that is to communicate in an honest way—straight from your heart. You can't go wrong with that. Let go of trying to make everything seem okay and make people "feel" good. If they are grown up, then you are not in charge of their feelings. Communicate in an authentic, truthful, human, and loving way.

Since we're on the subject of being human—one thing is certain, you will make mistakes. Even with your heightened awareness and new skills, you'll harm someone with your words. Dale Carnegie's Human Relation Principle Number Twelve states, *If wrong, admit it quickly and emphatically.* I've found one of my most effective communication tools is a genuine and sincere apology: "I am sorry. I did not intend it to sound that way. I apologize for speaking to you out of anger." Or, "I am sorry; my words were thoughtless and hurtful." That's how engaging leaders communicate. Contrary to any programming you may have received as a child, strong leaders demonstrate how to apologize and ask for forgiveness. That takes real confidence.

Don't Talk to Yourself like That

I can remember when both my daughters were younger. There were times when inevitably they'd speak harshly to their mom. My goal was to be mindful in these moments and intervene with, "Don't speak to your mother with that tone of voice. She doesn't deserve that. Apologize to her." I felt that it was important that they understood where acceptable boundaries were and be held accountable to honor them.

LISTENING TO THE EXPERTS

How do you foster relationships in your organization?

"The biggest thing about leading people…If I can get inside of a person's head and find out what makes him tick, I think the battle's over. You've got to find out what motivates a person. Everybody teaches it and everybody writes about it because it's the truth. Naturally, I can't get into the heads of five hundred salespeople, but I can get into the heads of twenty or thirty managers above them and find out what makes them tick. I do that before I hire most of them; I think it's a waterfall effect. They see what their leaders are doing, and they try to do the same thing.

"I'm very big on relationships with internal employees. It goes a long way if you can make people feel secure in their jobs, telling them, 'Hey, you're doing a good job!' or 'Hey, I like what you did last week; that was a great decision!' Before long, you can move away from managing them and go on to other activities, because I don't want to micromanage my people. A successful company requires leaders who can connect with their employees. It's just that simple."

—Marty Freeman, Senior Vice President
National Accounts, Old Dominion Freight Line

Since then it's occurred to me that we seldom hold our-selves accountable to the same set of boundaries when it comes to speaking to and about ourselves. Who protects us from ourselves? Who steps in on our behalf?

What does your ongoing "self conversation" sound like? You can't give to others what you don't give to yourself. How might you be committing verbal sabotage? If your internal language is beating you up all day, chances are you'll be sharing that same style with others who come in contact with you.

Begin to take charge of your inner dialogue. It's one of the few areas in life where you're actually in control. Become accountable to yourself by saying and thinking words that are positive and self-affirming. This may be the toughest communication assignment you've ever had.

Consider phrases like: "I am capable." "I have what it takes." "I have been created with unlimited potential." "I am designed for success." "I love myself." These words may sound silly and awkward initially, but it's probably an improvement over the thoughts you have been carrying around for the majority of your life. Protect yourself from your own destruc-tive words and take on a new self-talk vocabulary.

Be someone who builds up with your words. This doesn't mean you have to tell lies or use flattery. Whether it's with others or yourself, look for honest and genuine ways to see strengths and point out talents while providing insight and feedback that leads to greater success for everyone involved. In our next chapter I'll be disclosing a powerful tool that will have those you lead excited to hear your feedback and anx-ious to act upon it.

Recommended Action Steps

❖ Check your motives before throwing your truth at someone. More important than choosing carefully crafted words is your spirit behind those words. If you must speak a tough truth to one of your followers, be sure to serve it up with equal portions of love and kindness.

❖ Refuse to spin. Take to heart this advice from Emily Howard: "They're smart. They'll get it. Just say it." Your followers *are* smart. Speak the truth as you see it. You'll be respected as someone who is believable.

❖ Become aware of the words you think and say about yourself. Don't permit such negativity to be said about you by you. Speak and think words to yourself that are kind, honorable, noble, positive, and encouraging. You'll then be able to provide that same type of communication to others.

CHAPTER NINE

Crave Feedback

An unexamined life is not worth living.

– Plato

A few years back, I was conducting a learning workshop with a medical practice, and I arrived early to set up and connect with the attendees. There were about fifty participants, forty-five of whom were female nurses and staff. I paid particular attention to the attendees seated on the front row, realizing that I needed this group to be strongly on board with me. I began to build rapport with my front row team by asking their names, what role they played within the practice, how long they've been working there, and so on. It was going well with good conversation and intermittent laughter.

Moments before our workshop was to begin, I noticed one of the doctors stand up and begin to walk toward me. I thought, *This is good; he's the one paying my fee and probably wants to say hello before we start.* As we drew closer, he gestured for me to meet him in a private corner of the room. I mentioned to the ladies on the front row that I would be right back and at that time we'd begin our learning session. As I arrived at our private corner, the doctor leaned in, glanced around, and whispered, "Rich, your zipper's down."

Now that's feedback.

I took a quick look over at my front row companions, noticing strange looks on their faces and a reticence to reestablish eye contact with me. Was my sudden awareness uncomfortable? Yes! Uncomfortable for whom? Uncomfortable for everyone: the doctor, the nurses, and me. Yet think about it. How would I have felt three hours later, driving home, feeling a cool breeze and noticing my zipper was down? Did I like hearing about this awkward truth? No! Yet, I needed that information, and I needed it right then. I admire that doctor for having the courage to tell me what I was unaware of.

Your seventh fundamental principle is **Crave Feedback**. Feedback can be challenging. Often we recall experiences from our youth when we encountered feedback in an ineffective, unhealthy manner. Because of those experiences, we tend to shy away from that potential discomfort or avoid it altogether. Yet here's the bottom line: as an adult, your willingness to seek out and accept feedback from those you trust can be the difference between mediocrity and excellence.

Feedback is your personal GPS. It helps close the gap between where you think you are and where you actually are. It gives you a fuller truth to operate from and can offer perspectives that you might otherwise be blind to. At the workshop, I thought I was connecting and building rapport with my customers…and doing a good job of it. Instead, I was making people feel uncomfortable—not just for themselves; they were also uncomfortable *for me*. There was a serious gap, and someone needed to help me recognize that so I could fix it.

Actually, feedback cues are available to us all the time. They may be communicated verbally, or they may show up as body language. There are times we miss these signals entirely. In other instances, we receive the signals and choose to do nothing with them. Ultimately, we need a keen awareness to receive this valuable prize, the skill to deliver it, and the commitment to utilize it for the better.

Lost and Found

The great American philosopher Yogi Berra once said, "We're lost, but we're making good time." How apropos for today. Many of my clients are working harder than ever, yet they're not getting where they want to go. They utilize the power of feedback to help them get back on course. These trusted perspectives act as your personal GPS and can prevent you from going the wrong way…or correct your course and get you back on track for the journey.

It's not enough to occasionally stumble across accidental feedback. You've got to seek it and create a system to receive it as effectively as possible. Here are the three major components of a general feedback process:

People. Feedback is interactive, so you'll need people for this. But not just any people. Jesus had three (Peter, James, and John). Batman had one (Robin). Bonnie had Clyde, and the Lone Ranger had Tonto. He wasn't really "lone," then, was he? And neither are you once you build a team of allies. You need people around you who believe in you, who want you to believe in yourselves and achieve your own personal greatness.

Trusted perspectives act as your personal GPS and can prevent you from going the wrong way.

A good place to begin your feedback practice is with your peers. These are the people you can count on to be honest and unbiased. People you trust, those in your inner circle. This can be a gold mine for personal feedback, but it won't happen by accident; you must seek it out. It can be both uncomfortable and risky, but there is no substitute for it.

You also need feedback from those you lead. Currently, these may not be trusting relationships. That's okay. Eliciting their feedback can be a place to begin building trust. You can start by asking for their insight, listening intently, and then acting upon what you've discovered.

Format. Feedback can be more art than science, but there are guidelines that can make it more effective. Don't ambush someone by dropping the "I'd-like-some-feed-back-from-you" bomb and expect to receive an immediate response. Give the person an opportunity to prepare and think it over.

Try setting up an appointment for coffee. Tell her that you respect her thoughts and ideas and feel like she knows you well. Give her a specific scenario that you would like her to reflect upon. Choose from a personal relationship, a career decision, a financial issue, a health goal, and so on. Tell her what your desired outcome is and what you're currently doing about it. Then let her tell you what she "sees" from her vantage point.

Feedback is less dialogue and more listening for understanding. Ask clarifying questions that help you better grasp the recommendations. Like, *how do you think I could respond better in similar situations going forward?* Or, *where else do you see me behaving in this way?* The ground rules are simple. Anything that is said, any thought shared, any personal change recommended are all intended to make you better from their point of view. So it must be welcomed.

Response. Here's where you see what you're made of… and determine whether you get honest feedback again. If you're not ready to hear someone else's truth about you, don't ask. The worst-case scenario is to invite the process and then blow a gasket because you don't like what you're hearing. Be prepared to hear their truths without reacting negatively.

Resist the urge to make excuses. Pay attention to what resonates with you. What do you hear that makes you think, *Yes, I can see that, that makes sense*? Or, *I never saw that in myself. I was never aware of that.* If possible, a second opinion from another trusted friend can help solidify the areas upon which you want to improve.

Blind Spots

I had just dropped my youngest daughter off at volleyball practice. A sense of impending winter hung in the evening darkness as cold rain blew across my windshield. Deciding it was time to switch lanes, I checked my rearview and side mirrors—all clear. I hit my

Engaging leaders need "blind spotters" in their lives. Who are the people in your life that help you remain on course?

blinker and began nudging into what appeared to be an open lane. Instinctively, I took a quick glance over my right shoulder—whoa, headlights! A gentle jerk of my steering wheel placed me safely back in my lane. If not for that brief glimpse, I would have fell victim to the dreaded blind spot of driving.

After my heart rate returned to normal, my mind drifted back to earlier in the day. I was on my way to a noontime lunch meeting with my friend and business associate Emily Howard and a client. Just moments from my destination with an estimated time of arrival of 12:03, my phone rang.

"Where are you?" Emily questioned.

"I'm on my way. Where are you?"

"Waiting in the parking lot. Are you going to be late?" After a moment of silence, she asked, *"Can I give you some feedback?"* Although I trust Emily and am convinced she has my best interest in mind, I was still reluctant as I replied, "Sure."

She continued, "You're going to get a reputation of always running behind if you don't pay more attention to your timing."

In reality, I didn't like what I heard, even though it was on target. As the initial sting wore off, I became grateful for people like Emily who have the courage to tell me the truth so I can be better and live consistent with my vision. I didn't want a reputation for being late, yet there it was, sneaking up on me. It was in *my blind spot*, and I needed someone to help me swerve back into my lane—the lane of professionalism and timeliness.

Engaging leaders need "blind spotters" in their lives. Who are the people in your life who help you remain on course? What if you have no one in that capacity? Consider two possible reasons. One, you haven't asked or given anyone permission to serve you in that way. Two, someone has tried to help you with the inevitable blind spot, yet your response chased him away. Which of these fits you? What will you do about it? Don't let personal blind spots cause major accidents on your highway toward success.

How Are You Doing?

So, do you think you're doing okay? Do you think you're an engaging leader? Thinking is guessing. You either know the answer or you don't. One way to go from thinking to knowing is to consider a simple process that will allow you to engage in feedback with those you lead. As before, this is not a time to ambush the participant—no surprises. Set an appointment in advance, indicating that you would like to hear feedback from her regarding your effectiveness as a leader. Explain that your role will be to listen and take notes.

Begin by asking, "On a scale of one to ten, how would you score my effectiveness as a leader?[33] After listening to the response, ask, "Tell me why you gave me that score." After each answer or idea she provides, ask, "What else?" until she finally says, "That's it." Then ask the question: "What would have to be different for me to receive a ten?" Again, continue to listen and write the answers down, asking, "What else?" until she is done. Finish with one final question—"From the list of improvements you suggested, what do you see as my top priority?"

You will walk away from this encounter with extremely valuable information. Thank her for the gift of her insight and the courage to share her truth with you. At the end, tell her that you intend to make use of her thoughts and will later ask her again the same set of questions as a way to track your progress as an effective leader.

In *The Success Principles*, Jack Canfield writes:

Most people are afraid to ask for feedback about how they are doing because they are afraid of what they are going to hear. There is nothing to be afraid of. The truth is the truth. You are better off knowing the truth than not knowing it. And once you know, you can do something about it. You cannot improve your life, your relationships, your game, or your performance without feedback.[34]

As CEO of yourself, be receptive to the feedback that others have the courage to give you. Just as with the feedback received from trusted friends, treat this as the gift that it is.

As CEO of yourself, be receptive to the feedback that others have the courage to give you.

Be sure to do something with it. Allow it to sink in and create time for quiet introspection. What truths are staying with you? Have you had similar feedback in the past? What resonates with you? What should you let go of? The best return gift you can provide your feedback provider is to follow up and let her know what her words have done for you and how you've benefited.

Giving Effective Feedback

The Bible talks about "speaking the truth in love."[35] Feedback is that way: it must be delivered and received as both truth and love. The truth alone is never enough; you can give people truthful feedback but care less whether they actually improve or not. That's where love comes in. As important as it is to deliver truthful words, the spirit behind the words is equally important.

I receive ongoing feedback from Chris Avis—college roommate, one-time business partner, and longtime trusted friend. Sometimes it hurts, and sometimes it feels good. What makes it most powerful is that it is his truth, delivered in love. I remember two specific incidents where Chris did this for me.

Years ago, I was struggling to understand what was preventing me from really connecting with people on a deeper, more intimate level. I was sharing this concern with Chris while he was sitting in my office. He looked right at me and remarked, "I never worried about losing you as a best friend. I knew you would never let anyone get close enough to you." *Ouch!* That didn't feel good. Yet it resonated with truth. I had indeed kept people at a distance for years, afraid to let them get too close. I had made an agreement with the lie that if others knew my faults and imperfections, they would reject me. Chris had given me a gift of truth, delivered in a private moment when I was open and needed to hear it.

More recently, Chris and I were at Outback Steakhouse enjoying conversation, a cold beer, and some large slabs of beef. He said, "Of all the people I know, you are the one who should be great." Wow. Talk about impact. Both times, he gave me feedback that I will never forget. Both were equally important truths delivered with love. He wants me to succeed. He wants me to be great, to fulfill my potential, and to reach my dreams. That's what real feedback can do for you.

LISTENING TO THE EXPERTS

How do you create a culture of feedback among your people?

"Our president travels a lot to our branches, and one of the things he's doing this year, just to foster this kind of engagement, is to have a coffee hour or social with anyone who wants to come and talk. He's not coming to give a presentation on the state of the union but to check in with them on how they're doing. It's not pre-scripted; it's, 'I'm available and want to know how you're doing. Where do we need to improve?' Conversation, it's not any more complicated than that.

"Part of our culture is what we describe as 'loose tight.' We encourage new ideas and entrepreneurship. For example, last month in Lynchburg, Virginia, we opened an occupational medical clinic; that idea came from clients and employees, not the president and leaders. In short, there was a vacuum in the marketplace for businesses with workers' compensation claims. Instead of having to go to the ER, they needed an occupational medical clinic. So on February 9 (and it took a year and a half of planning and hard work), we opened. My point is that we've engaged our employees now; we want them bringing ideas and opportunities for how can we serve our clients better. Hey, the crazier the better."

—Brett Grieves, Vice President
Scott Risk & Insurance Services

Trust Yourself

Do you know that you can offer yourself feedback? That's right. You have an ongoing conversation in your head all day, every day. You even have that dialogue at night. We have a name for that—dreams. Your mind and heart never shut down, so it's time to take control of that conversation and use it for good.

I remember when my daughter Taylor was in my room talking about some things that were important to her. Now, my girls know that I have strong feelings about cell phone interruptions. It drives me crazy when people stop interacting with a person right in front of them and respond to the ringing of their cell phone. Our priorities can get seriously screwed up.

Yet during this conversation with Taylor, my cell phone rang…a call I had been waiting for. So I took the call. A few moments later, Taylor whispered, "I'm going to bed, Dad. Love ya." I smiled, blew her a kiss, and continued to laugh and focus on my call. Later that night and early the next morning I couldn't get that interaction out of my head. Or my heart.

Lacking the opportunity to gather feedback from a friend, I decided to conduct a personal debrief. I asked myself what might be causing this inner conflict, and it became crystal clear. I had demonstrated exactly what I don't like about choosing technology over people. My actions were incongruent with my beliefs. No excuses—I blew it. So I went back to Taylor, telling her how important it is for me to be with her and what an honor it is to listen to her. I explained to her how bad I felt about choosing my cell phone call over her. I apologized and told her it wouldn't happen again. None of that learning could have happened if it weren't for some time of self-reflection and honest self-feedback.

Self-feedback requires moments of quietness. It can happen while driving in your car, first thing in the morning, late in the evening, or at a special place where you can be alone with your thoughts. Begin by "debriefing" your day. What events stand out to you? What interactions occurred today? How do you feel about them? What do you think about them? If you could go back and change anything, what would that be? Why?

Feedback is priceless—and rare. Ultimately, to be highly successful, you must learn how to give and receive it effectively. If you listen to those you trust, it will act as a guide to your journey. When you give it, make sure you do so with truth and love. It will make you a better person and an engaging leader.

Now, in our next chapter, let's consider how the skill of creating fun impacts engagement.

Recommended Action Steps

❖ Within the next thirty days, schedule a time to receive feedback from someone you trust. Choose a specific life area (e.g., personal relationships, leadership style, business relationships with peers, etc.) and give him or her time to prepare. Perhaps share the "On a scale from one to ten" model outlined in this chapter. Be prepared to listen, ask clarifying questions, take notes, and act upon the ideas you hear.

❖ Within the next thirty days, schedule a time to provide feedback for one of your direct reports. Follow the same format. Deliver it with truth and love. Be prepared to support him or her in making the necessary changes as a result of your conversation.

❖ Carve out some quiet time to listen to your own thoughts. Focus on a specific event from the previous day. Ask yourself, *how did that turn out? What could I do different and better next time? What can I learn about myself from this experience?* See what you have to say about and to yourself. Be truthful, kind, and loving.

CHAPTER TEN

Have Fun

There is work that is work, and there is play that is play;
there is play that is work, and work that is play. And in
only one of these lies happiness.

— Gelett Burgess

One of my favorite childhood memories is a joke my mom would tell: Two adult brothers lived at home with their mother. One of them had a cat that he worshiped; he treated the cat like a child. One day, he decided to take a short vacation by himself. He asked his brother to look after the cat. "You know this cat means the world to me; please take good care of her while I'm away," he implored. Shortly after he arrived at his hotel in Florida, he called to check in. "How's Kitty?" he asked.

"She's dead!" replied his brother.

Sorrowfully, he responded, "You know how important she was to me. Why couldn't you have broken the news a little more gently? Perhaps on my first call, you could have told me, 'She's up on the roof and can't get down.' Then, on my next call you could've added, 'She fell off the roof and we took her to the veterinary hospital,' and so on." He angrily hung up the phone on his insensitive brother and returned to his hotel room distraught. The next day, feeling a little better, he called his family to check in again. When his brother answered the phone, he said, "Sorry for getting so upset yesterday. I just loved that cat. So, how's Mom?"

The brother responded, "She's up on the roof and can't get down!"

That was my mom's favorite joke. Usually we would be in the car, and she would begin telling the joke like none of us had heard it before. We would look at each other with the expression that said, "Oh boy, Mom's telling the joke again; she must need a good laugh." My dad would shake his head, grip the steering wheel tighter, and apply a little more pressure to the accelerator.

Now, here's the strange part. My mom would never finish the joke. Midway in, she would start giggling. Then she would slide into a heavy chuckle, leading to full out laughter, building into a body-shaking, head-bobbing outburst that climaxed with her gasping for air and her mascara running down her face! I kid you not.

My brothers and sisters and I did not laugh at the joke; we had heard it too many times. What we did end up laughing at was my mom. Although I would try to talk her down as soon as I sensed it coming, the effort was always unsuccessful, and I would end up laughing in amazement at Mom's teary, unfinished joke. My mom, a very successful professional with advanced college degrees, knew how to have fun and understood the power of a good laugh.

Does Misery Really Love Company?

It's time to consider your eighth fundamental principle: **Have Fun**. I refer to this as the corporate "F" word. When I mention the importance of fun, it's often met with gasps as if I'd just let out the original "F" bomb. It seems to me that most corporate settings are asylums for misery. It rarely appears as if people are having fun and enjoying their experience. This is evident when I ask acquaintances, "How do you like your work?" More often than not, this question is followed by a deep sigh and a dejected, monotone voice that answers "Twelve more years." I didn't know they were incarcerated.

Growing up, two of my favorite TV shows came on late Sunday afternoons. They were *Wild Kingdom,* followed by *Wonderful World of Disney*. Life was good! *Wild Kingdom* was all about these manly men entering the wild habitats of dangerous creatures, and the goal, it seemed, was always the same. Shoot the wild boar or cougar with the tranquilizer gun, check its teeth for potential gum disease, tag its ear, and release it. It was dangerous and exciting work. When asked, "How do you like your job at Wild Kingdom?" I bet they never sighed and responded, "Twelve more years." Recently, I have had a personal fantasy. It's a twist on *Wild Kingdom*, and it goes like this: I don some authentic khaki safari gear and load up a tranquilizer gun. Next, I head down to the local corporate office park. I then

It's time to choose your attitude!

bust into the first organization I find, tranquilize the inhabitants, check their teeth and gums, tag their ear, and release them from their imprisoned misery! Now, because we've tagged their ears, we can track them to better understand the migration habits of miserable employees.

Here's my only concern: I worry that they will end up returning to a different corporate location, only to be trapped in the same type of unhealthy, repressive, joy-sucking habitat. There seems to be a misery pattern for people. That's what they're accustomed to and that's what they'll put up with. This fantasy has a sad ending. I return to my Jeep, sweaty and dejected.

When did we start accepting the idea that our careers had to be devoid of fun, meaning, and inspiration? Let's get this corporate revolution started (or revival...you choose what to call it). In Victor Frankl's *Man's Search for Meaning*, while recalling his imprisonment in a Nazi concentration camp, he writes, "Everything can be taken away from a man but one thing: the last of the human freedoms—to choose one's attitude in any given set of circumstances, to choose one's own way."[36] In corporate America, it is time to choose your attitude.

What's Your Role in This?

Maybe fun is the real "F" word in our corporate jungles. It's not that you have to be a standup comedian or make balloon animals for your people; I'm not talking about creating a false or shallow environment. Life is funny enough. The universe supplies all the material you need to laugh and have fun on a daily basis. Just look around and pay attention: life is funny!

Think about the people you know who enjoy what they do. What makes it that way for them? Now let's get personal—do you have fun with your work? Why do you enjoy what you do? When you do the work you're intended to do, the work that is placed within your heart, it's fun. Even when it's tough and challenging and pushing you outside of your comfort zone. The fun you're having should radiate from you towards those you lead. It's contagious and they'll catch it.

Are you celebrating the good things that are happening? Do you smile when you walk through your business and greet others by name, or are you too busy with really important stuff? To put it bluntly, *Are you having fun yet*?

We spend too much of our lives at work to be miserable there. As leader of your life, do you find meaning and joy and excitement in what you do? Do you transfer that energy and enthusiasm into the "wild kingdom" of your office? Dare to bring fun back to corporate America. People will thank you for it.

Don't Take Yourself So Seriously

It's okay to take your work seriously, but try to lighten up on yourself personally. Sam Walton founded and developed the world's largest retailer (Wal-Mart). He also danced the hula on Wall Street in a grass skirt in 1984 after his organization turned in an exceptional year.

On a cool autumn day in October, I pulled up to the corporate offices of my client, Window World. This was my first official visit to its North Wilkesboro, North Carolina headquarters. As I opened the door to enter, two things captured my attention. One was the warm greeting on a sign in the lobby reading, "Welcome Rich Schlentz." The other was the receptionist sitting behind the desk in a Halloween clown outfit. I had heard Jacqueline's voice before and had experienced her personal, professional demeanor on the phone. But this was our first face-to-face encounter. My response was laughter, comfort, enjoyment, and

❖ ❖ ❖

Leaders need to be pushed out of their comfort zones and allow themselves to have fun.

❖ ❖ ❖

engagement. From that moment I was convinced that Window World was a fun place to work...and I was right. It also sells more windows each year than any other company in the United States. Think there might be a connection?

I was recently gathering some feedback from a group of professional speaking peers. We took turns critiquing new material each of us had developed. Part of the presentation I was practicing had the audience repeating a chant aloud after me. One leadership consultant spoke to me personally after my review was complete. He said that the chant might not go over well if I was speaking to a room full of leaders. They might feel uncomfortable and resist my urge for them to participate.

I considered his feedback for a few days after I had received it, and here's my conclusion: I will keep the chant. For the exact reason that it was suggested I remove it. Leaders need to be pushed out of their comfort zones and allow themselves to have fun—even look silly at times. If it's good enough for Sam Walton, it's good enough for the rest of us.

Bah, Humbug...

Wondering how all of this connects with business results, growth, and profits? Mary Rau-Foster discusses Dr. David Abramis' studies at Cal State Long Beach on fun in the workplace:

> [Abramis has] discovered that people who have fun on the job are more creative, more productive, better decision-makers, and get along better with co-workers. They also have fewer absentee, late, and sick days than people who aren't having fun.

The benefits to a pleasant and happy workplace are that happy employees are more loyal and productive employees. The absenteeism and tardiness rate may decrease as people look forward to going to work. The turnover rate may decrease, as employees feel content and loyal to an organization. And the cost associated with illness may decrease as people experience the positive physiological and psychological effects of laughter.[37]

So why isn't there more of it? Why do the majority of workplaces seem to be a Petri dish full of grumpy, impersonal, and negative cultures? Recently, while working with a team of managers, they concluded that both positive and negative attitudes are contagious...yet the negative ones spread more rapidly. When we discussed why that might be, here was our conclusion: it takes no special skill or abilities to be negative. Therefore, negativity flows easily and unencumbered from one person to the next. In contrast, a positive and fun-loving attitude calls for skill, energy, and intention. That's why it's rare. Ya got what it takes?

Your Customers Feel it Too

Asheville, North Carolina was a beloved vacation spot for my wife and me. In addition to enjoying the mountain air, local cuisine, and talented street musicians, one of our favorite pastimes in Asheville was to visit the eclectic mix of art galleries and museums. It was while visiting two different art galleries that we witnessed first-hand what it truly means to create an engaging and fun culture. It was an experience I'll never forget.

LISTENING TO THE EXPERTS

How do you keep your company from getting too stuffy and stiff?

"It started probably year four or five: we had a watermelon seed spitting contest for accuracy and distance. We played Taboo®. We've made paper airplanes and tested who could keep them afloat longest. Because we work with rubber bands a lot in preparing mail, we had accuracy contests, shooting into a target with rubber bands. We've gotten away from that in recent years, and we need to get back to that culture where we aren't taking ourselves so seriously all the time. I think I started focusing on the more serious issues, but I think a serious issue is how do you have fun at work? Tomorrow we have eight different people bringing a crock-pot of chili, and without labeling whose chili is whose, we're going to taste it and vote for our favorite. A lot of folks are excited about it, and the winner gets fifty dollars to take to a restaurant of their choice. I think that's a small way to keep people engaged. We go to the Greensboro Grasshoppers ballgame as a company; we've done that for about three or four years in a row now. We're going to do a picnic this year—we haven't done one of those for a few years. Bottom line: I want this to be a fun place to work."

—Jeff Burkett, President
Advanced Direct Inc.

After purchasing our tickets at one museum gallery, we were handed a pamphlet listing eleven sacred guidelines designed to "help make your visit more enjoyable." Among those:

- Please do not touch the walls, frames, or glass.
- Please do not stand too close to the artwork.
- Please do not point at the artwork.
- (And, our favorite, the puzzling…) Please go outside to ride your Segway.

The staff stealthily hid behind desks rather than interacting with visitors, yet they appeared out of nowhere to scold me for violating one of their commandments (as I inadvertently placed my hand on the wall to read the description of a piece of art). I can imagine their staff meetings bogged down with conversation focused on the latest protocol for adhering to the rules and regulations—now that sounds inspiring and fun. No wonder when it came time for my wife and me to leave, we felt bored and uninspired. We half-heartedly joked about asking for a refund of our money and the hour of wasted lifetime we'd never get back.

What a contrast that was to our experience at the Jonas Gerard Fine Art Gallery. Upon entering their inviting, bright gallery, we were greeted by Gerard's original work and several signs that boldly stated, "IT'S OK TO TOUCH." He had a world map with the question, "Where are you from?" Alongside was a box of colored pushpins. The map was covered with hundreds of multicolored pins representing visitors and customers from across the globe.

We were delighted when, moments later, the white-bearded, raspy-voiced Gerard entered the gallery and began interacting with visitors. Throwing back his head and shaking with hearty laughter, he took the time to display various works under special lighting and discuss the pieces with those gathered round him. Following Gerard's lead, his staff was delightful. We exchanged names as we walked and chatted about art and our life journeys. Later, he gamely posed for a picture with my emerging-artist wife and spoke personally with us for thirty minutes. Yet, our conversation had little to do with his artwork.

It's hard to imagine that these polar opposite experiences were both created intentionally!

Instead he encouraged my wife, Ivy, to pursue her love of art as a healing modality for her stage-four breast cancer. He breathed inspiring words into Ivy about artistic expression and surviving cancer (himself a sixteen-year survivor of larynx cancer), causing tears of belief and gratitude to well up in her eyes and cascade down her cheeks. The experience left us feeling inspired with a renewed sense of well-being.

It's hard to imagine that these polar opposite experiences were both created intentionally. These two galleries reflected vastly different organizational cultures: one was upbeat, energetic, creative, and fun. It honors people and interacting with them. The other was blank, barely alive, focusing on rules and regulations. Sadly, many people exist in similar soul-sapping, process-focused environments for a majority of their working lives. In these cultures, greater respect is given to the hallowed pages of the Employee

Policy and Procedure Manual than to the employees themselves.

The formula for an engaging culture is amazingly simple yet dishearteningly rare. People before product. Interaction over procedure. Jonas Gerard gets it. Focus on people and your product flows out the door. The stodgy museum approach is wallowing in a model that's out of touch with people and wholly focused on its product. As customers, I won't be purchasing any more eight-dollar tickets to visit the museum gallery again. In honor of Ivy, and our experience together, I plan on spending much more than that to someday display a Gerard original within my home. Fun is a good business strategy.

Bill Gove writes, "Success is more of a subtraction process than it is an additive process. We already have all we need inside of us. Success is simply a matter of removing the beliefs, attitudes, and habits that get in our way."[38] The same can be said for fun. What belief, attitude, or habit needs to be removed so that you can start having some fun?

Just say no to the corporate agony, and begin your own personal revival. Decide that fun has a place at work. Then get some of your own—others will catch it from you. Fun inspires…and inspiration is the topic of our next chapter.

Recommended Action Steps

❖ Make an honest assessment of the fun factor in your workplace. Are you allowing and nurturing this type of culture? Simply walk around. Listen. Pay attention. What do you see, hear, and feel? Is anybody having fun? Write down what you observe.

❖ Determine to have more fun. Make a list titled, "Fun things I like to do." Then schedule at least one of those events in the next thirty days. Reclaim your right to have fun. Spend more time with friends (or strangers) who know how to have fun and break up with your joy-sucking friends. Identify which is which.

❖ Find out how your customers feel about your product or services. Does the thought of interacting with your staff get them excited, or do they dread the experience? Ask them. Listen to what they have to say. If they're having fun and are uplifted by you, your team, and your product, they will gladly part with their money over and over again to replicate the experience.

CHAPTER ELEVEN

Inspire Them

If you want to build a ship, don't gather your people and ask them to provide wood, prepare tools, assign tasks. Call them together and raise in their minds the longing for the endless sea.

— Antoine de Saint-Exupery

When I asked the audience about a line that was most memorable from the movie *Jerry Maguire*, most of the men shouted, "Show me the money!" while the women simultaneously exclaimed, "You had me at hello!" It's interesting how these responses generally run down gender lines. Yet there's one line in the movie that speaks to us all. It has to do with a fundamental concept that transcends gender, ethnicity, and generations. Let's set the stage.

The movie begins with Jerry Maguire stowed away in a hotel room, seemingly under a spell or curse. He can't sleep. He's caught by a belief that there's a better way to represent athletes as a sports agent. This compelling vision won't leave him alone—he can't shake it. It's like an ocean riptide from which he is unable to free himself.

Excitedly, Jerry compiles his ideas into a document and presents it to his peers at the agency. To his dismay, only one loyal colleague finds value in Jerry's vision and commits to accompany him on his adventure. Together, along with the office pet goldfish, they begin their quest to work under a new paradigm.

Shortly into their launch, business is slow and tensions high. The stress causes Jerry and his lone supporter, Dorothy Boyd, to be at odds. That's when I heard her say it, the phrase that we all believe but few ever articulate: "I care about the job, of course, but mostly, I just want to be inspired." Each time I watch the DVD, I blurt out, "Preach it, sister, preach it!" Isn't that the case? Don't we all want to be inspired?

Most of us are conscientious. We've been taught to provide an honest day's work, do the right thing, and respectfully deliver a satisfactory return on investment to our employer. Yet deep down inside, we hear our inner thoughts whisper, *There's got to be more to it than this.* We hope and pray that someday our work will actually inspire us.

Henry David Thoreau had it right when he penned, "The mass of men lead lives of quiet desperation."[39] Lack of inspiration comes at a price and causes people to retreat into lives of fantasy football, reality TV, and infomercials. Instead of living and working a life of adventure and meaning, people seek artificial means to fill the hole left in them. Dan Miller writes about it this way:

Each of you is creative, innovative, intelligent, and passionate. Yet often only a small portion of your unique talents are tapped.

> Given the amount of time we spend working, failure to find meaningful, significant work is not just a minor misstep in living out God's plan; it is a deeper

kind of failure that can make each day feel like living death.[40]

Employees all across this globe have a deep desire to be part of meaningful work that brings fulfillment to their lives. They are not asking that this be delivered to them on the proverbial silver platter. Rather, they are willing to work for it and bring their skills and talents to the table of endeavor.

Each of you is creative, innovative, intelligent, and passionate. It's how you're created; it's part of your being. Yet often only a small portion of your unique talents and gifts are tapped into. That can leave much of you dormant, uninspired, and underutilized. It is time to address this shortfall. That's why your ninth fundamental principle is **Inspire Them**.

The Uninspired Experience

Nothing subdues inspiration more that meaningless words and actions. Let's begin with *meaningless words*; this describes most corporate mission statements spot-on.

Have you read your corporate mission statement lately? And? What does it say to you? What does it mean to you? How does it inspire those you lead? Who wrote it? Chances are good that if you are not its author, it means and speaks nothing that moves you. As a matter of fact, mission statements have become comedic in many organizations—an example of how out of touch leaders can be.

One of my clients has a running joke about his organization's executive leaders, who spin corporate words and phrases, dropping them down the elevator shaft like a sack of flour. Through these mandates and orders they hope to create the magical "buy-in" (which itself is a meaningless corporate phrase that sounds better than its frequent intent: manipulation) necessary to establish belief and support for their initiatives.

When will we learn? People want to be heard. Have you listened to what your people are saying? Is what they say reflected in your organization's mission, vision, and values? Does it resonate with them? Does it speak to their souls and hearts? Does it inspire them?

Your stockholders aren't the ones who are slugging away day in and day out for greater efficiency, productivity, and profitability. Stockholders aren't required to deliver innovative and creative solutions that grow revenue and lower costs. If you've written your company mission statement with the stockholders in mind, then you've missed the mark. They don't need inspiring words; employees do. Give the words in your mission statement a long, hard look—then make the necessary changes so it can become the inspiring document it's designed to be.

Now let's consider the impact of *meaningless action*. We often disguise this under the heading of "goals." Sometimes they're dressed up a little and called "stretch goals." Goals void of vision are nothing more than a call to work harder—without a sustaining and compelling reason to do so. Your people are looking for ways to connect their "doing" with their "being." Goals or action steps alone aren't enough. Sure, receiving a paycheck might act as a short-term stimulus for achieving a goal, yet we know that even a paycheck can't keep a person inspired over the long haul.

While we're on the topic of compensation, money doesn't equate to inspiration. Researcher Amy Wrzesniewski states:

The most recent evidence suggests that money is losing its power as a central motivator, in part because the general population is realizing, in greater numbers, that above a minimum level necessary for survival, money adds little to their subjective well-being.[41]

More and more we are seeing people who will choose a highly engaging culture over a higher paying offer, demonstrating the bottom-line value of meaningful work and relationships. We are also observing that employees caught in cultures without inspiring and meaningful work can be lured away at practically any price. Let's discuss how you can transform this dynamic by inspiring the people you lead.

Meaningful Words

What cultivates inspiration? The right words crafted into a short, compelling statement of purpose. The courage to see and speak an inspiring future into our people. In *Leading With A Limp*, Dan Allender writes:

The difference between a manager and a leader is the internal urge to alter the status quo to create a different world. In that sense leaders are prophets. They see the present as incomplete and inadequate and are willing to risk the comfort of the present for the promise of a better tomorrow.[42]

At times we all need someone who imagines what can be, could be, and should be. Someone who can conjure up a future ideal state and communicate it with clarity and power.

143

In other words, occasionally we all need to be in the presence of, or to be, a prophet.

There are a number of ways to communicate vision. Often we call them purpose, mission, or vision statements.

❖ ❖ ❖

When the right words are delivered with authenticity and vision, then those words can move people to action.

❖ ❖ ❖

When the right words are delivered with authenticity and vision—when the ideas elevate our collective hope for the future—those words can move people to action. Here's one of the best purpose statements I've ever read. My clients at The Decal Source in McLeansville, North Carolina, wrote this: *Our mission is to succeed with our partners as we maintain a healthy balance between work, family, and God.*

What makes a statement powerful and inspiring? Truth. Clarity. These are meaningful words that accurately represent the people at The Decal Source. How does your company or department's purpose statement measure up? Why does your company or your department exist? Connecting with its soul—determining its purpose (see chapter 1)—is critical for an inspired work culture.

This is a tough assignment. It requires deep thought. You may have to get in a quiet place to ask yourself or others the *Why do we exist?* question. There are a number of formats or templates you can use. One that I have found to be effective is in Jack Canfield's book, *The Success Principles.* Go ahead and get started thinking about, articulating, and writing your organizational and personal purpose statements; your life and work are too important not to be on purpose.

Here's my personal purpose/mission statement:

My purpose is to inspire others to discover, embrace, and put into practice their God-given talents. I do this through the use of my gifts: humor, emotion, enthusiasm, and sincerity. What once seemed ordinary is now EXTRAordinary! Courage overcomes fear, love and laughter abound, judgment is reserved, and people are living on purpose.

My company purpose statement is even simpler: *EXTRAordinary! Inc. is a movement dedicated to reviving the global workplace, one culture at a time.*

These words speak to me. The words I've chosen are powerful, positive, and present tense. I recite these statements each morning to remind me why I'm here and why I do my work. These carefully chosen words remind me to keep my actions and purpose aligned—now, that's inspiring!

Purposeful Actions

We can inspire purposeful actions when we connect goals with vision. History is inundated with examples of amazing acts of bravery that were fueled by a clear purpose. What caused people like Gandhi, Martin Luther King, William Wallace (of *Braveheart* fame), Mother Teresa, Jesus the Christ, and others to leave their mark on our entire planet? Where did they conjure up such courage in the face of overwhelming odds? How did they continue moving forward when their very lives were at risk? Simply put, they acted on purpose.

LISTENING TO THE EXPERTS

How do you inspire your people?

"This is my fundamental promise to the people that I hire: Number one, you will grow professionally as a result of being employed by this company. Number two, I will commit to share the financial success of this company with you in the future. These are two fundamental things that I said in the beginning, and I've done both. In fact, if you were to call one of my employees right now and say, 'Tell me about Larry's two fundamental promises to you?' they would recite these to you. You can call anybody in my office, and he or she will recite it to you. And it's worked."

—Larry Diana, Owner
Express Employment Professionals

Their missions were crystal clear. An independent India. Civil rights for all races. Freedom from oppressive rule. Provision for the poor. A spiritual message of good news and abundant life. Their daily actions were directly linked to their vocational purpose. Can you connect the actions that you and your employees take on a regular basis to a purpose greater than yourselves? When you do that, motivation will no longer be an issue.

I mentioned earlier that my first career was in the health and wellness industry. One of our top salespeople was a woman named Dawn who had a gift of genuine concern and care for others. Coupled with her sales acumen, she was a formidable force for our organization.

One afternoon a prospective member came into our main facility. The best way I can describe him was old and grumpy. At times like these I was especially pleased to have people like Dawn to engage our potential members. I did not have the patience to deal with Mr. Grumpy. But Dawn did, and she helped sell another membership.

As it turned out, Mr. Grumpy had a number of physical challenges and chronic diseases, and to assist him with these ailments, his son accompanied him to each exercise session. Dawn kept a close watch over this gentleman, making sure that his workouts went smoothly and that all his needs were met. She even had our fitness department purchase a wheelchair that was kept at the building entrance. When Mr. Grumpy's son drove up, she'd make sure that one of our staff met them at the front door, checked them in, and escorted them to the men's locker room.

This went on for several months. Mr. Grumpy was making progress and even gained enough energy to have an important surgery completed. He would be out of commission for several weeks and then back to his exercise regimen. After that respite, Mr. Grumpy's son appeared at our front desk, carrying a potted flower in full bloom. He asked our receptionist to page Dawn, and since I overheard the request, I offered to go find Dawn in her office.

Dawn was young, attractive, and full of energy, so it was not unusual to have potential suitors track her down at our facility. When I approached Dawn and described the situation, she was visibly frustrated; she didn't have the time to politely shoot down another love interest. But there was no way out, and she was forced to face the young man.

Dawn took a deep breath, smile intact, and headed toward the reception desk. And here's what Mr. Grumpy's son said: "Hi, Dawn. This is for you. My dad didn't make it through his surgery. I wanted you to know what an impact you had on his quality of life these past several months. He was happier than I had seen him in a long time. You really made a difference. Thank you for all you've done."

Wow! What a moment that was for all of us. It was in this experience that the real meaning of Dawn's work crystallized. She wasn't in sales. She wasn't even in the health and wellness business. She was impacting the quality of people's lives. She was making a difference. And Dawn never looked at her work the same again. Her actions were purposeful and meaningful because she was inspired. Simple and profound.

Infectious Passion

Reggie sang in church recently. It was moving. It's not that Reggie has a flawless voice or that he hits every note with perfect pitch. It's something else that causes your spirit to stir and your body to sway when Reggie sings. It's passion. Reggie sings with unbridled passion, and it's absolutely contagious. That's probably what caused the entire congregation to stand up and some to shout, "Come on, Reggie. Yes, Reggie, sing it now!"

I've had similar experiences watching jazz bands play on the patio of Cheesecakes by Alex in downtown Greensboro. I love to watch the bass players in particular; there's just something about bass players and their facial expres-

Her actions were purposeful and meaningful because she was inspired. Simple, but profound.

sions. They are passionate. It's as if they are all alone. No audience—only them, their bass, and the music. Often their eyes are closed, and their head is bobbing to the beat. It's an intimate dance between them and their instrument, and I feel like they are allowing me into a place that's typically private.

All this reminds me of the author's notes in the book *Blue Like Jazz* by Donald Miller. He writes, "Sometimes you have to watch somebody love something before you can love it yourself. It is as if they are showing you the way."[43] Passion is powerful. Passion is moving. Passion is inspiring and can show us the way.

Recently, I was conducting a yearly strategic planning session with my client, Kathie Johnson, president of Thomasville Medical Center. Kathie put together the event to recognize her team for all they had accomplished during the prior year and to involve them in creating a vision for the upcoming year. When it came time to generate new initiatives that would help fulfill their vision, Kathie was the busiest person in the room, furiously writing down all of the ideas. Engaging leaders bring passion to their work.

Kathie believes in the medical center's organizational purpose: helping patients heal, easing pain, offering hope, providing comfort, and supporting families. And Kathie's passion is contagious. You could feel the energy spread throughout the room, inviting her team into the freedom of dreaming and thinking big. The result was several flip chart pages full of meaningful ideas, plans, and initiatives. Kathie's passion made you love strategic planning. She was showing the way.

What about you? What passion do you bring to work? How do you demonstrate your love of life? In what ways does your passion "show the way" for those who follow you? If Reggie can do it, if bass players can do it, if Kathie can do it, then so can you. Give yourself permission to unleash your passion in the workplace. Be the spark that ignites the souls of others.

Discover, Embrace, and Utilize Your Strengths

Corporate America has spent entirely too much time and money on weakness. It seems to be enamored with it…but that's stupid. Spending all our time between annual reviews painfully sweating over weaknesses causes people to disengage. It is suicide for the soul. *Stop it*, I tell you—*stop it right now*. This is not for you.

Linda and I were at our weekly coaching session. She's a manager at a local medical practice, and our goal for this session was to review an assessment she had completed that named her dominant strength themes. As we discussed the assessment outcome, I acknowledged how her strengths played a powerful role in her success with the current challenges she was facing. I paused as the tears began to roll down her cheeks. She wiped her eyes with a tissue and said, "I've never focused on my strengths before. I never really knew I had any."

What a shame—and what a common experience. You see, like most people in the workplace, Linda was keenly aware of her weaknesses. Indeed, they had been pointed out for most of her life, and as a result, she was hyperconscious of where she failed. Through a weakness-centered development focus, she had hit a barrier in her career; weaknesses had paralyzed her. What she needed most was to be introduced to her strengths and her unique abilities. Linda needed to understand how to focus on and utilize her strengths in a way that created successful outcomes for her.

I'm not suggesting that we should ignore our weaknesses. I am saying that the corner on that market is secure. We get that part! We've heard about all our lacks and limitations for most of our lives. It has been well documented—sealed in our permanent files like a ticking time bomb. Now is the opportunity to give equal opportunity to discovering, embracing, and utilizing the traits that will lead to our success, not our demise. This is the approach that releases energy and fuels accomplishment.

Engaging leaders know their own strengths, and they know the strengths of those they lead. Engaging leaders build a successful and inspiring culture by focusing on and applying those strengths. Good-bye, weakness-focused workplace. Rest in peace.

Tell Your Story

We were on a family vacation one summer in Vermont. The kids were young, so we decided to stop at the iconic Ben & Jerry's corporate headquarters on our return trip. This was the proverbial "win-win," as the children would get ice cream while I'd get a close look at a highly successful business model. We'd all be happy.

What they did best that day was tell their story!

Until this point, I had never purchased a Ben & Jerry's product. "Too expensive," I would mutter. We pulled up to the Ben & Jerry's factory (yes, it is a manufacturing facility) and guided the excited children through the parking lot toward the "Tour Entrance" sign.

After paying our admission fee, we mingled around a gift shop before hearing the cowbell announce our tour departure. All along I was thinking what an amazing idea the company had developed: it had created a revenue stream from people coming to see their production plant. (Isn't capitalism wonderful?) The tour was insightful, entertaining, thought provoking, and educational. Employees on the production floor below us stopped and waved as we walked on by. We finished by sampling some free ice cream flavors and hanging out in a children's play area. What fun to experience the joy on my daughters' faces as Cherry Garcia, Chunky Monkey, and Cake Batter ice cream dripped off their chins. That might have been the moment they became lifelong loyal consumers of Ben & Jerry's.

For me, what they did best that day was *tell their story*. The tour was really about understanding who Ben and Jerry were. They were common, everyday people like us. We learned about where they grew up, their personal values, and how they intended to keep their company aligned with those values. It didn't matter whether you agreed or disagreed—you had a better understanding of who they were and where they were coming from. Their story was simple and powerful, and I became a believer.

After that visit, I too was a loyal customer of Ben & Jerry's ice cream. I no longer felt that it was overpriced because I wasn't just buying ice cream; I was supporting my belief in that story. These two guys morphed from slick marketing images into real-life people. People like me that I could relate to. Since business is about people and relationships, I felt connected to their product in a way that I didn't feel connected to Haagen Dazs or Breyers. And all of that happened through the power of story.

When I teach presenters how to be more engaging, I start by encouraging them to weave stories into their speeches. At some point I often hear, "But I don't have any good stories." Yet that is never the case. We all have good stories. It's just that some have realized the power of their stories while others haven't.

Good stories come from everyday life. They take the shape of lessons you've learned growing up. They sound like accomplishments you've achieved throughout your life. They are the challenges you've faced and overcome. They can be joys you've felt and sorrows you've experience. Stories are about you and your journey and your beliefs.

What makes a story inspirational is your willingness to define it and the courage to tell it. By "defining" it, I mean giving proper attention and honor to your unique story. To help uncover some of your own story, ask yourself these questions: *What brought me to this point? What has shaped me along the way? What have I learned from a particularly challenging experience? How has it impacted me? What do my business and I stand for? What's important to me? What am I passionate about and why?*

In the book *The Leader's Voice*, the authors state, "Hucksters tell great stories. Leaders tell *their* stories."[44] Give your story some attention. Define it. Have the courage to speak and write about it. What is the story behind your company? Your common, everyday story will end up inspiring others to follow you because they'll understand where you've come from, who you are now, and why it's important that you keep moving forward.

Inspiration Is A Choice—Make It Yours

You have a chance to create an inspiring culture, a culture that resembles what Patanjali, the compiler of the Yoga Sutras, described here:

> When you are inspired…your mind transcends limitations, your consciousness expands in every direction, and you find yourself in a new, great, and wonderful world. Dormant forces, faculties, and talents become alive. You discover yourself to be a greater person by far then you ever dreamed yourself to be.[45]

Why would you not do this? So much of our lives are committed to work that it should be a place that inspires us to our core. You deserve this. Those you lead deserve it. After all, you care about your job, of course, but mostly, you just want to be inspired.

Recommended Action Steps

❖ Assess your company or team's level of inspiration. Ask several of your people, "On a scale of one to ten, how would you rate the level of inspiration here?" Then ask, "Why do you give us that score?" Followed by, "What would have to be different or change for us to get a ten?"

❖ Reevaluate your purpose, mission, and/or vision statements. Do they resonate with those who follow them? Are the words meaningful and inspiring? If not, consider gathering your team and updating the statements with them.

❖ Speak your company's story to others. Remind them of why the work you do is important. Crystallize the core values of your organization through stories that demonstrate them in action. Next time you have an opportunity to speak before your group, inspire them with your corporate journey story—where the company has come from and where it's going.

CHAPTER TWELVE
Buckle Up

The door is open but the ride ain't free.
                                    – Bruce Springsteen

This was my senior high school picture and quote from Bruce Springsteen's song "Thunder Road." As I think back on that phase in my life, I surprise myself. Perhaps I was more aware and intuitive than I have given myself credit for. This phrase was published shortly before leaving New Jersey and moving five hundred miles south to follow a dream of winning a national championship soccer title. Apparently, I inherently understood that this door open to me would carry a price. All worthwhile adventures in life do have a cost—they're not free. That's what makes them valuable. This journey you've undertaken to become an engaging leader comes with its own price as well.

Along with most high school seniors, I had friends sign my yearbook. I noticed that a frequently reoccurring phrase was, "Don't ever change." As in, "Rich, good luck in college next year. Have a great summer. Stay the same and don't ever change." I've reflected back on that oft-used saying and cringed. What if that had been the case? What if I had indeed never changed? What was meant as a kind sentiment would have become a lifelong curse—the "high school yearbook curse."

Without my own personal change I would have had no chance of evolving into the person I am intended to become. I would have been destined to remain an eighteen-year-old blockhead forever. So it is with you and all engaging leaders. Change, better yet transformation, is the only way—and that ride ain't free.

From Change to Transformation

Change is hard. We've all experienced that personally and professionally. People naturally tend to cling to "sameness," to the known. Entire cultures have emerged around keeping things as they were. There's an illusion of safety or comfort that this provides. But this is not for you. You must not only be willing to change, you must also be committed to journeying through the door of transformation.

In his book *Spiritual Liberation*, Michael Bernard Beckwith discusses the difference between change and transformation. "Change occurs when something shifts in our consciousness along with a corresponding behavior change. Stopping an addiction is change. Although if we regress in consciousness, old patterns may reassert themselves."[46] Here's the liability with change: It's not permanent. Change has a limited shelf life because it sprouts from human will. It focuses on outward "behavior" and not the internal programming or belief system that drives corresponding behavior or action. Therefore, it's a battle of "wills," consuming a lot of energy with sporadic results, leaving individuals and teams often feeling exhausted and defeated.

On the other hand, Beckwith states, "Transformation is limitless since it stems from an evolving discovery and expression of the Authentic Self." With transformation, there's no going back because it's "a movement of awareness away from limited thought forms into a conscious realization of our limitless nature. Transformation gets us free."[47]

Have you ever seen a discontented butterfly? The caterpillar is not focused on change; it's yielding to the butterfly within as the acorn yields to the oak tree within. It's transforming into its original design and fulfilling its earthly purpose—there's no returning to the caterpillar state. The caterpillar didn't complete a self-improvement program or a change management workshop. It didn't "will" itself to make the butterfly happen. It simply allowed its natural path to occur. It transformed and in the process accomplished its intended purpose.

Did this require effort? Was there a cost? Yes…yet not as we typically measure effort or cost. The real trick here is willingness to yield. Transformation is less about hard work and more about being clear on what you are designed to become. It's less about pushing something to a desired result and more about being pulled along toward a purposeful, intentional outcome.

The caterpillar didn't complete a self-improvement program or a change management workshop!

Transforming into your very own intended engaging leader is the journey to yourself. It is the passionate pursuit of becoming who you and your business are intended to be. Simply, it is fulfilling your purpose. Don't settle for change when you are destined for transformation. Have the courage to do the work necessary to live your purpose as an engaging leader—you won't regret it.

The Way of an Engaging Leader

This process can begin when you are willing to sit quietly with yourself and gain insight. When you trust yourself, believe in yourself, and even love yourself. When you're willing to yield to the gifts, talents, and greatness that reside within you. This can be a challenge because this way of thinking, of believing, is often contrary to the lifelong teaching of lack and limitation to which many of us have been subjected.

The way of the engaging leader is abundance. When you arise in the morning, do you worry yourself about a potential lack of oxygen? Do you conserve your breath in an effort to protect against an impending shortage of air? Do you recite a silent prayer, pleading for the opportunity to experience a full day of breathing? No. You simply take it in. Accept it. Receive it. Make good use of it.

I went hiking in the North Carolina Mountains recently. I rested beside a creek at the base of a thunderous waterfall. Sitting upon a fallen tree spanning the body of water, I was mesmerized by the sight and sounds of the water rushing over the edge of the falls. As long as I sat there, water kept flowing. Never ceasing. Relentless. How many years had it been doing this very thing? How much longer would it continue? I found myself wondering about its source, as the flow of crisp, cold mountain water was constant, seemingly endless. So it is with you. Your ability to engage your work and personal life knows no limits. It is up to you to open the floodgates and let the "water" flow. Here are some suggestions that will help you tap into the source of abundance that awaits you as an engaging leader.

You Will Want to Remain. Go.

My mom taught me a lot of lessons growing up. She was a lifelong nurse and educator, so she required all of her children to learn CPR and first aid in our home. We grew up thinking that all kids had a CPR mannequin in their closet! Since my mom worked with hospice, we also learned about dignity in dying and death. I can remember her talking with her colleagues about how important it was for the family of a hospice patient to "give permission" to their family member to die. I often heard her say that individuals would try to survive longer and resist dying if they felt that the family still needed them or was uncomfortable with their impending death. In April 1996 we were celebrating my mom's sixty-seventh birthday with friends over for Easter Sunday. Simultaneously, my mother was preparing to transition as a result of lung cancer. My sisters, brothers, and I could see she was fading fast; a week

We often think of love in terms of remaining. My mom taught me about the type of love that is willing to go.

after our celebration, she began her dying process. She had lost the ability to communicate verbally, yet we knew she was still coherent. One afternoon several of us kids spent some time around her bed, telling old stories, laughing, and crying.

Eventually, it came time to head into the living room and give Mom some peace and quiet. On the way out of her bedroom, the lessons she had taught me years before came flooding back. I stopped, turned around, and approached her bed. Bending over, I put my hand on her forehead and whispered into her ear, "Mom, we're gonna be okay. When you're ready, please go. I love you." Two days later, she passed on.

We often think of love in terms of remaining or staying put. Yet my mom had taught me about a different kind of love, the type of love that's willing to go. Maybe that's the kind of love you need right now—a love that releases. It's time for you to go…to move toward your calling. You're not doing anyone any favors by remaining as you are. Your opportunity as an engaging leader, as part of the movement to revive the global workplace, awaits you. You need to go now. We need you to go now. It is time.

You Will Want to Hold On. Let Go.

I once read this story in the *Shambhala Sun* magazine. The name of the article was "Here, Now, Aware: The Power of Mindfulness," by Joseph Goldstein:

> In some Asian countries there is a very effective trap for catching monkeys. A slot is made in the bottom of a coconut, just big enough for the monkey to slide its hand in, but not big enough for the hand to be withdrawn when it's clenched. Then they put something sweet in the coconut, attach it to a tree, and wait for

the monkey to come along. When the monkey slides its hand in and grabs the food, it gets caught.[48]

If we were to ask the monkey, "What has trapped you?" he might answer, "This darn coconut has me trapped!" or perhaps "This tree has caught me!" You don't have to be any smarter than a monkey to blame your predicament on circumstances or surroundings. But you are smarter than a monkey. As an engaging leader, you take 100 percent responsibility. You can see that the monkey has caught himself. The solution is clear. Open his hand, release the treat, slip out, and be free. Only a rare monkey will actually do that.

Are you really smarter than a monkey? Oftentimes I find that people are trapped by their refusal to let go of the very thing that has them caught. They create their own personal imprisonment, denying their freedom to grow and develop by holding on to past programming, thoughts, beliefs, emotions, habits, ideas, feelings, or people that should be turned loose and sent packing. Therefore, they ultimately prevent themselves from moving toward their calling as an engaging leader.

I'm not suggesting you pretend that certain circumstances, issues, or feelings never happened. I'm recommending you acknowledge them for what they are, respond with the appropriate emotion, and then release them—not remaining trapped in the wake of your past. There is a Taoist saying: "Knowledge is learning something new every day. Wisdom is letting something go every day."[49]

You Will Be Caught by the Old. Choose the New.

I recall a time when I was a child. I had just created a mess by spilling my bowl of cereal. Without thinking, I said to my mom, "Uncle Roy is right. I am trouble." These words originated from the way my favorite uncle would often welcome me into his home, "There's Richard. Here comes trouble." Unconsciously, I had made an agreement with his voice—the programming—and created a truth, then I began to operate out of that belief system: *I am trouble.*

The next time we visited Uncle Roy, my mom marched up to him and ordered that he cease calling me "trouble" because I was beginning to believe it. That's how it works. Here's the good news: since you're grown up now, you get to choose the thoughts and beliefs that suit you best. That means becoming aware, listening to yourself, and letting go of old, worn-out thought patterns that no longer serve you.

You can choose your own programming and create new beliefs that tell you the real truth about yourself.

You get to choose the thoughts and beliefs that suit you best, letting go of old, worn-out thought patterns that no longer serve you.

Here are ten ways to help you accomplish this:

1. Create a personal purpose statement and life vision (see *Success Principles* by Jack Canfield, chapters 2 and 3). This reinforces the belief in who you really are and where you are headed.

2. Pay attention to your thought patterns. What current beliefs do you recognize regarding your success, finances, confidence, relationships, health, and so on?
3. Schedule regular time for silence and thoughtfulness—begin to recognize, acknowledge, and listen to your intuitive voice.
4. Journal. Write something down about your life experiences as often as you can. Ideally, a few sentences per day. You are not being graded—spelling and sentence structure don't count.
5. Spend time with people who inspire and encourage you while provoking new thoughts. "Fire" those people who drain your energy and discourage you.
6. Ask people you trust for feedback. (See chapter 8.)
7. Read. Check out my website resource page for recommendations at extraordinaryinc.com.
8. Listen to inspirational music or personal development messages while driving.
9. Limit your time watching TV and reading the newspaper.
10. Engage in activities that inspire you: gardening, sports, exercise, writing, theater, art, music…whatever moves you and makes you feel more alive.

You Will Fall. Get Up.

A few years ago, I was updating my yearly vision. While listing goals under my health and well-being category, I decided that this was the year to act on a dream I had had for a long time: competing in a triathlon. It was finally time for this idea to be materialized.

After ordering a book on triathlon training and determining a location for swimming, I took my bike out of storage to have a tune-up performed. With tune-up complete, it was time to mount the bike and reacquaint myself with long-distance cycling using my clip–in pedals.

These pedal systems are crucial for triathlon competition, as they provide the power necessary to cover long distances as efficiently as possible. But it takes some coordination and getting used to, as your feet are securely locked into the bike pedals using special shoe cleats.

Stopping at traffic lights and stop signs can be particularly challenging with these cleats. I had created a system to ensure my safety, always stopping in the right lane, unclipping my right foot, and balancing on the right hand curb. This process had proven effective on my inaugural rides.

At the conclusion of my third training ride in this new triathlon season, I was preparing to make a left-hand turn that leads into my neighborhood. Encountering a red light, I stopped in the left turn lane, unclipped my cleat, and placed my left foot on the concrete median. As I was in the habit of doing, my weight shifted to the right. I could feel the sensation of my body as it slowly tilted right, lifting my left foot from the security of the solid earth. As I approached the upright position, a brief thought traveled through my mind, *I am going to fall flat onto the left-hand turn lane. I'm not even moving—falling while at a complete stop is not cool. What type of story can I make up to tell my friends that won't sound so dorky?*

And that's pretty much the way it happened. A few seconds later I lay flat on the road, right foot still firmly attached to my pedal, pinning me under my bike. I was flopping around like a fish out of water, attempting to release my right cleat, climb out from under my bike, and regain my upright position as quickly as

A few seconds later I lay flat on the road, right foot still firmly attached to my pedal, pinning me under my bike.

possible—all while trying to maintain some semblance of coolness. After what seemed like an eternity on the asphalt, I was finally free, upright, and kneeling next to my bike, inspecting it like some mechanical error had occurred instead of obvious rider incompetence.

As I look back, I had a question to answer only moments after freeing myself. That question was, *Will I get back on my bike?* In actuality I had several options. I could trash the whole idea, utilize the infamous phrase, "I guess this just isn't meant to be," walk my bike the short distance home, and place it back into storage. I could change my goal to competing in a duathlon—specifically swimming and running, since both of those activities seemed safer and provided softer landings for me. Or, I could get back on my bike, complete the ride, and continue triathlon training. Without a second thought, I climbed back on my bike and rode home with a bruised right hip and ego.

The moment of falling is not the time to make a critical decision like this. As a matter of fact, your answer to the question about getting back on your metaphorical bike should be established prior to your inevitable fall. My answer was decided when I was working on my visioning process. As a result, a few days later I was on the bike, clipped into my cleats, enjoying the feeling of wind and freedom rushing over me.

Three months later, I was competing in my first triathlon. After that exhilarating event I stuck around for the award ceremony to soak up some of the pomp and circumstance, post race food, and the energy of other athletes. As winners were announced over the PA, I heard the master of ceremonies call, "First place in Novice Masters Division…from Greensboro, Rich Schlentz!" Holy cow—I had won my class! Not bad for a guy who falls while standing still at an intersection with his bike.

Falling is part of the process for an engaging leader. It is often the result of resorting back to old habits. Make your decision to get back up long before you fall. Be kind and compassionate to yourself. Continue your journey. Ice your bruises and encourage your spirit. Revisit your purpose, vision, and goals—they are too powerful for you to stay down. You owe it to yourself and to those you lead to follow through. Get back up… I'll see you at the awards ceremony.

You Will Doubt. Believe.

Motivational speaker Les Brown states, "Sometimes you have to believe in somebody's belief in you until your belief kicks in."[50] When Ivy was alive, I would often find myself propped up by her strong belief in my ability to be a highly successful consultant, speaker, and writer—waiting for my own belief to kick back in.

What gets in the way of your self-belief? Doubt. Where does doubt have its origin? Similar to our "Let go" discussion earlier in this chapter, doubts are an indication of our belief system. They are "blockers," preventing us from going forward. They take the form of voices and conversations in our head that impact our course of action. Let's spend a little time on these.

It was an early spring morning, and I was driving west toward Asheville, North Carolina, and the Blue Ridge Parkway. I had planned this hiking weekend for months; it was part of my vision. Time alone. Three days of thinking, listening, and writing. For many years I had hurried along with my life, often distracted by the menial tasks that consumed my thoughts and energy. I had allowed myself to be surrounded by society's "noise" until my own inner voice was no longer audible. Herman Melville said, "Silence is the only voice of our God."[51] Armed with a vague idea of my destination, I was going to find out if Mr. Melville knew what he was talking about.

It was a misty morning on the Blue Ridge Parkway; at times, the fog was so thick that the posted forty-mile-per-hour speed limit was dangerously fast. Luckily, there were few other drivers sharing the winding roads and steep drop-offs with me. I approached my first potential stopping point at Crabtree Meadows

Soon after pulling into the parking area, it became clear that the trail-hiking season had yet to officially begin: all the buildings were locked with a prominent sign stating, "CLOSED." No helpful park rangers or other hikers were to be found. In fact,

Doubt can be just like that—conversations in your head that won't quit. Their ultimate calling is to immobilize us.

there was a barrier blocking the road leading from the parking area to the trailhead. The message coming across was loud and clear: leave! But I had not traveled all this way to turn back now. My vision was still clear and inspiring. I was here for a purpose, I reasoned, so I pulled my gear from the car, suited up, and marched onward.

Moments after clearing the roadblocks and power walking toward the magical trailhead, the heavy mist turned into a full-fledged rain. This was not the "picture" I had been holding in mind. Not the cool April morning, sunshine warming my spirit, Carolina blue skies that I had imagined. It was cold, gray, dreary, and now…raining! I paused momentarily to look back at my car while it was still in sight. Its warm, dry interior was inviting, to say the least.

Right then, on the solitary Blue Ridge, I became keenly aware of a boisterous and annoying conversation erupting in my head. The voices seemed to keep pace with the increasing precipitation, and the words racing in my head took on a familiar sound. The scene was eerily similar to that of my family at Thanksgiving dinner while growing up in New Jersey: everyone talking loudly, no one listening.

Doubt can be just like that—conversations in your head that won't quit. They live rent-free in the inner cities of your mind, rarely interested in a dialogue, perfectly happy in their all-consuming monologue. Their ultimate calling is to immobilize you—to pull you back to the warmth and safety of your comfort zone.

In this particular instance I was able to momentarily quiet the inner noise, pull my baseball cap down more snugly around my head, and raise my windbreaker collar up around my neck. I glanced once more at my car, turned, and pressed on.

Here's what the voices of doubt sounded like on that day: "What made you think you could pull this off. You know you're not a planner—figures this place would be closed. You should've known things would fall through. You didn't even check ahead to see if this trail was open. It takes someone smart and savvy to execute a successful adventure like this. Well, at least you can tell people you gave it a try—always good to have an excuse when you fail. You're a hopeless dreamer."

Doubts can also sound like the voices of others. It may be a parent, a relative, a coach, or a teacher from early in your life. Those authority figures may have told you what you could or could not accomplish. They may have even convinced you of who you should or shouldn't become. All doubts become self-defeating thoughts. Here are a few of the more common doubt phrases; place a check mark next to the ones you recognize as having used before:

__ It's too difficult.

__ It's too risky.

__ I'm too busy.

__ I'm too old.

__ I'm too young.

__ I'm too clumsy.

__ I'm not good enough.

__ I'm not smart enough. I don't have a degree.

___ I'm not handsome or pretty enough.

___ I can't afford it.

___ I'm afraid.

___ I don't have time.

LISTENING TO THE EXPERTS

How did you make a choice for engagement?

"In 1974 there were three owners at Scott, and they decided they wanted to retire and sell the company. Instead, they decided to sell the company to the employees. It was a huge turning point when those three decided not sell out to a stranger but to sell to the people who made the company what it was. That big step in our history has helped our people be engaged. Think about it: Every person walking the halls owns the company! So engagement isn't difficult here; it's not a job anymore. This ownership structure is a blessing, and as a result, we're a very transparent company. All the employees see the financial data; we have shareholder meetings; we pay dividends. So they're treated as owners, and this has created a uniquely engaging culture for us."

—Brett Grieves, Vice President
Scott Risk & Insurance Services

Doubt Busters

Doubt's biggest fear is that you might act upon your inner calling. Doubtful thoughts resist your growth and inhibit your God-ordained journey. They prefer well-worn recliners, conversation about the weather, and familiar TV reruns. But it's time to banish doubt from your head and heart.

Begin to take charge of your inner conversations. Refuse to default to the voices and lies that have taken squatter's rights inside you. How can you do this? First, become aware of what is being said in your thought conversations. Next, start speaking new truths to yourself. Here are a few phrases you can adopt for reprogramming your thought life:

- I am brilliant—a pure genius.
- I am creative and innovative.
- I am unlimited potential.
- I am unlimited abundance.
- All that I need to succeed already resides within me.
- I am an engaging leader.
- I am courageous.
- I am more than enough.
- I am confident and strong.
- I am worthy; I deserve this.

These new thought phrases might feel silly or embarrassing at first—that's because you're more familiar and comfortable with your self-demeaning inner voices. If you make the effort to instill these new thoughts, you'll initiate a life-altering experience. Which beliefs will you choose? Old lies or new truths? You decide. It's time to be different. Quiet your doubt, change your inner conversation, be the engaging leader that already resides within you, ready to emerge through and as you.

What should you expect as a result of all of this work? What will be the result of your transformation into the engaging leader you are destined to become? Perhaps the authors in *The Leader's Voice* say it best:

> If you choose to lead, prepare to take a stand. It is not for the faint–hearted. Some will judge you unfairly, blaming you for their lack of success. Others will expect resources you cannot give, answers that you do not have, and permission you cannot grant. You will be misquoted. Your judgment will be questioned. You will certainly stumble. Failure will stalk you like a predator...The toughest problems will be yours alone. You must take responsibility for your failures and give credit for the successes. Lose the fantasy that you will be cherished, immortalized, and revered. Expect long hours and few moments of gratitude.
>
> Expect also that some will soar beyond your expectations. They will create magic inspired by your dreams. They will make you glad you chose to lead. They will hear what you say, understand it, care about it, and act. Together, you will engage in the best work of your lives.[52]

There you have it: expect pain and joy. In other words, you will feel more alive than you ever have before. There is a cost, but the return on investment is priceless.

The Heart of the Matter

There once was a very prosperous and successful king. For centuries, the royal family had held a secret from their loyal subjects: they were keepers of the key to happiness. After so many years, the king was fearful that the people of his great kingdom would learn of his family's prized possession and, if found, use it unwisely.

One morning the king summoned his brightest and most trusted sage to help solve this dilemma. "Bury the key to happiness in the deepest ocean," proclaimed the sage.

"No, my subjects would surely dive to the depths of the sea to find it," replied the king.

"Hide it on top of the highest mountain," was the sage's next recommendation.

"No, I know my people—they will climb relentlessly and discover the key there," said the king.

"I know," said the sage with confidence, "Bury it deep within each of their hearts. They are sure to never look there to find it."

I first heard this fable about a year ago, and its truth rings loud and clear. It reminds me of the lesson embedded in the *Wizard of Oz* metaphor—the simple truth that all you need to be successful, all that's required to live your purpose and be fulfilled, lies within you. Whether it's courage, a heart, or a brain—it's all there. You lack nothing. Neither the wizard nor the king can touch what's inside of you. You decide whether your "keys" remain hidden and dormant…or discovered and activated.

Wayne Dyer wrote, "True nobility is not about being better than anyone else. It's about being better than you used to be."[53] This is the journey to your true nobility, the journey to your heart. The journey to yourself—the person you're designed to be, called to be. This is your road to becoming an engaging leader. Let's continue to walk it together.

Endnotes

1 Rodd Wagner and James K. Harter, *12: The Elements Of Great Managing* (New York: Gallup Press, 2006), xiii-xv.
2 Ibid, vii.
3 This idea comes from Rob Bell, *Velvet Elvis: Repainting the Christian Faith* (Grand Rapids: Zondervan, 2005), 11.
4 John Lennon and Paul McCartney, "Revolution" (EMI Music Publishing/Sony ATV Music Publishing LLC, 1968).
5 Jack Welch and Suzy Welch, "A Healthy Company?" *BusinessWeek*, podcast, May 3, 2006, http://www.businessweek.com/mediacenter/podcasts/welchway/welchway_05_03_06.htm.
6 *The Free Dictionary*, "Engagement," http://legal-dictionary.thefreedictionary.com/engagement
7 John Fleming and Jim Asplund, *Human Sigma: Managing the Employee-Customer Encounter* (Washington, DC: Gallup Press, 2007), online excerpt at http://gmj.gallup.com/content/102496/where-employee-engagement-happens.aspx.
8 John Gibbons, "Employee Engagement: A Review of Current Research and Its Implications," *The Conference Board* (November 2006), http://www.conferenceboard.ca/documents.aspx?did=1831.
9 *Mark Sanborn*, "Strategic Execution," blog entry by Mark Sanborn, November 9, 2009, http://www.marksanborn.com/blog/strategic-execution/.

[10] *Think Exist,* "Johann Wolfgang von Goethe Quotes," http:// thinkexist.com/quotation/knowing_is_not_enough-we_ must_apply-willing_is/209797.html.

[11] Pete Townshend, "Who Are You?" (MCA Records, 1978).

[12] Katherine Sharp, as referenced by Sarah Ban Breathnach, *Simple Abundance* (New York: Warner Books, 1995), 80.

[13] Dan B. Allender, *Leading With A Limp* (Colorado Springs: WaterBrook Press, 2006), 3.

[14] Dewey Bunnell, "Tin Man" (Warner Bros. Records, 1974).

[15] Iyanla Vanzant, *One Day My Soul Just Opened Up* (New York: Fireside, 1998), 116.

[16] Bruce Springsteen, "Born to Run" (Columbia Records, 1975).

[17] Bob Nelson, "What Matters Most Isn't Money," *New Mexico Business Weekly,* January 17, 2003.

[18] Staci Eldredge, *Captivating* (Nashville: Thomas Nelson, Inc., 2005), 138.

[19] "A Little Enlightened Self-Interest," *Inc. Magazine,* June 2010, 60.

[20] John Eldredge, *Journey of Desire* (Nashville: Thomas Nelson, Inc., 2000), 62.

[21] *Emmanuel Oluwatosin*, "Teachers Open Doors...But You Must Enter Yourself," blog entry, September 2, 2009, http:// www.eolutosin.com/pursue-your-dreams-2/.

[22] Steven Pressfield, *The War of Art* (New York: Grand Central Publishing, 2002), 122.

[23] Dan B. Allendar, *To Be Told* (Colorado Springs: WaterBrook Press, 2005), 122.

[24] Foundation for Inner Peace, *A Course In Miracles, Combined Volume* (Wisconsin Dells: New Christian Church of Full Endeavor, 2005), 631.

[25] Victor Frankl, *Man's Search For Meaning* (New York: Pocket Books, 1959), 17.

[26] John Moyne and Coleman Barks, *Open Secret Versions of Rumi* (Boston: Shambhala Publications, Inc, 1984), 8.

[27] See John 8:32.

[28] John G. Miller, *The Question Behind the Question* (New York: G. P. Putnam's Sons, 2004), 97.

[29] Rob Bell, *Velvet Elvis*, 28.

[30] *PHNet.fi*, "Ralph Waldo Emerson Quotes," http://www. phnet.fi/public/mamaa1/emerson.htm.

[31] Dan B. Allender, *Leading With A Limp*, 180.

[32] Pat McCloskey, "Where Did St. Francis Say That?" *American-Catholic.org*, October 2001, http://www.americancatholic. org/messenger/oct2001/Wiseman.asp.

[33] Jack Canfield, *Success Principles* (New York: HarperCollins, 2005), 157.

[34] Ibid, 158.

[35] Ephesians 4:15.

[36] Victor Frankl, *Man's Search For Meaning*, 86.

[37] Mary Rau-Foster, "Humor and Fun in the Workplace," *WorkplaceIssues.com*, 2000, http://www.workplaceissues.com/ arhumor.htm.

[38] Consistently Great's Weblog, "Bill Gove on Success," blog entry by consistently great, September 12, 2008, http:// consistentlygreat.wordpress.com/2008/09/12/bill-gove-on-success/.

[39] Henry David Thoreau, *Walden* (Boston: Beacon Press, 1997), 6.

[40] Dan Miller, *No More Mondays: Fire Yourself—And Other Revolutionary Ways to Discover Your True Calling at Work* (Colorado Springs: Waterbrook Press, 2008), 2.

41 Rodd Wagner and James K. Harter, *12: The Elements of Great Managing*, 114.

42 Dan B. Allender, *Leading With A Limp*, 58.

43 Donald Miller, *Blue Like Jazz* (Nashville: Thomas Nelson, Inc., 2003), ix.

44 Boyd Clark and Ron Crossland, *The Leader's Voice* (New York: SelectBooks, Inc., 2002), 110.

45 *Think Exist*, "Patanjali Quotes," http://thinkexist.com/quotation/when_you_are_inspired_by_some_great_purpose-some/326077.html.

46 Michael Bernard Beckwith, *Spiritual Liberation* (New York: Atria Books, 2008), 29.

47 Ibid, 29.

48 Joseph Goldstein, "Here, Now, Aware: The Power of Mindfulness," *The Shambhala Sun*, November 2007.

49 Margaret Meloni, "Knowledge and Wisdom," PositiveArticles.com, n.d., http://www.positivearticles.com/Article/Knowledge-and-Wisdom/50469.

50 "NMPRO #254—Les Brown Interview 3 of 4," *Network Marketing Pro*, March 3, 2010, http://networkmarketingpro.com/2010/03/03/nmpro-254-les-brown-interview-3-of-4/.

51 Herman Melville, *Pierre* (New York: Penguin Books, 1996), 208.

52 Boyd Clark and Ron Crossland, *The Leader's Voice* (New York: SelectBooks, Inc., 2002), 14–15.

53 Wayne W. Dyer, *There's a Spiritual Solution to Every Problem* (New York: HarperCollins Publishers, Inc, 2001), 135.